Sustaining Your Well-Being in Higher Education

T0372822

This book provides an evidence-based approach to sustainable self-care, anchoring these strategies in individual academic workers' core personal values. It teaches readers how to use their values to leverage self-care strategies into a workable, individualized, and effective map to wellness.

Working in the demanding environment of higher education can leave little time for self-care, yet making space for wellness and self-care is essential to creating a creative and innovative environment for academic work. This book shows how to create and successfully implement realistic self-care plans. By identifying core values and using these to develop individualized self-care plans, *Sustaining Your Well-Being in Higher Education* pushes back against a one-size-fits-all approach while also discussing the role of self-care in academic labor activism and providing strategies for readers to become advocates for better self-care practices within their zones of influence.

Designed to provide academic workers with the skills they need to develop workable and sustainable self-care plans, this book is an invaluable resource for students and professionals working in all areas of higher education.

Jorden A. Cummings, Ph.D., is Professor and Clinical Psychologist who researches and disseminates effective self-care practices. Dr. Cummings lives, works, parents, and plays on Treaty 6 territory in Saskatchewan, Canada.

Wellbeing and Self-care in Higher Education
Editor: Narelle Lemon

For more information about this series, please visit www.routledge.com/Wellbeing-and-Self-care-in-Higher-Education/book-series/WSCHE

Sustaining Your Well-Being in Higher Education

Values-Based Self-Care for Work and Life

Jorden A. Cummings

Routledge
Taylor & Francis Group

LONDON AND NEW YORK

Designed cover image: © Getty Images

First published 2025
by Routledge
4 Park Square, Milton Park, Abingdon, Oxon OX14 4RN

and by Routledge
605 Third Avenue, New York, NY 10158

Routledge is an imprint of the Taylor & Francis Group, an informa business

© 2025 Jorden A. Cummings

The right of Jorden A. Cummings to be identified as author of this work has been asserted in accordance with sections 77 and 78 of the Copyright, Designs and Patents Act 1988.

British Library Cataloguing-in-Publication Data
A catalogue record for this book is available from the British Library

Library of Congress Cataloging-in-Publication Data
Names: Cummings, Jorden A., author.
Title: Sustaining your wellbeing in higher education : values-based self-care for work and life / Jorden A. Cummings.
Description: Abingdon, Oxon ; New York, NY : Routledge, 2025. | Series: Wellbeing and self-care in higher education | Includes bibliographical references and index.
Identifiers: LCCN 2024014851 | ISBN 9781032460376 (hardback) | ISBN 9781032460369 (paperback) | ISBN 9781003379805 (ebook)
Subjects: LCSH: College teachers--Mental health. | College teachers--Job satisfaction. | College teaching--Psychological aspects. | Well-being. | Self-care, Health. | Work-life balance.
Classification: LCC LB2333.2 .C86 2025 | DDC 378.1/25019--dc23/eng/20240529
LC record available at https://lccn.loc.gov/2024014851

ISBN: 9781032460376 (hbk)
ISBN: 9781032460369 (pbk)
ISBN: 9781003379805 (ebk)

DOI: 10.4324/9781003379805

Typeset in Galliard
by KnowledgeWorks Global Ltd.

This book is dedicated to Morley, my essential why.

Contents

List of Figures

List of Tables

Prologue

Jorden A. Cummings

It's Fall 2010. My first few months in a new job in a new province. While technically it's still Autumn, that's somewhat meaningless in Saskatoon – we already have snow. It's getting dark earlier and earlier, and the sun is coming up later and later. I had no idea this happened here, and I am beginning to feel claustrophobic from the lack of light. I have an apartment on the 21st floor of a building downtown, with large windows overlooking the river and a desirable neighborhood called Varsity View. I'm standing at my giant windows, looking at the lights of all the houses (in the freaking dark, even though it's not even 6 pm!). And I am crying.

I'm crying weird tears. On one hand, I'm crying because I feel so fortunate and relieved to have finally "made it". I am a shiny, brand-new Assistant Professor on the tenure track. This was the dream, and I achieved it (or so I thought). All my brutal, bloody (literally... I once stapled my fingers together in the lab), tear-filled, anxiety-ridden mental-health-sacrificing work has paid off. Right?

I am also crying because I am utterly exhausted, from my mind to my organs to my bones to my soul. Every morning, I drag myself out of bed. I love working at home, but after my department head comments one day that she has been trying to catch me in my office, but I'm never there, I am filled with anxiety and drag my ass to campus every single day. I come home from work, and all I can do is watch television and cuddle my cats – feeling guilty the entire time because I "should be working". I don't recognize this as burnout because... it's the first semester of my new job. How could I be burnt out already?!

I am 29 years old. I am overwhelmed. No one told me how much recovery time getting a PhD requires. I am ~2 years from finding out I have a chronic illness (the first of several), and I am 14 years into my journey with chronic depression. And I am not prepared for how academia will chew me up and spit me out over the next decade.

Today, as I begin this book (Fall 2022), I am twenty days shy of my 42nd birthday. I have recently been promoted to Full Professor and am an entirely different version of myself. Or I am *more myself* than I have ever been. My life looks mostly the way I always wanted it to. I know who I am. I know what's important to me. I am proud of my accomplishments – academic and otherwise. I am proud of persevering in creating space for my inherent right to well-being.

Thinking about that new 29-year-old Assistant Professor crying in her apartment – alone in a new city with no friends, no interests besides academia, and an existential crisis on her hands – it brings tears to my eyes. As I write this, I am drinking coffee and sitting in a conference room with nine women at a writing retreat. I am calm and not frazzled (today, at least). What do I owe this change to? My personal and professional journey with self-care.

Over my first year on the tenure track, my exhaustion from graduate school became my determination to do my career (and life) differently. I was sick of working all the time, sick of not looking after my physical or emotional health. I was lonely. At some level, I already realized what I wouldn't come to vocalize for almost another decade: I won't survive if I continue living my life like this.

That year began my personal and professional deep dive into self-care – I had dabbled as a graduate student. Still, my Ph.D. program didn't exactly encourage self-care (despite whatever they believed they were doing, which is what pretty much every other graduate program is doing). As a new tenure-track professor, I did what any academic would do: I turned to the literature to tell me what to do. It didn't take very long for me to realize "The Literature" was…. suboptimal. Although there were some gems, much of what was published on self-care at the time was opinion, advice, or editorials. This hasn't changed much in 14 years. And while advice is great, I was a hardcore positivist then. I wanted experiments. I wanted randomized control trials. I wanted an evidence-based guide for What The Hell I Should Be Doing besides grinding away my body and soul on the tenure track. I wanted theory.

Moreover, a lot of the advice assumed that people like me lacked *knowledge* about self-care. The writers seemed to believe that if they could just tell me a laundry list of things I should be doing, I would have an epiphany and overhaul my life. "Why is it", I wondered, "that self-care writers assume I don't know what I should be doing?"

I'm an educated person. I'm a *helping* professional. I knew I should exercise, relax, eat vegetables, and maybe meditate. My problem wasn't the lack of things I could try but finding the time to do them. It was figuring out which of them I wanted to do and how to fit them into my life. It was setting boundaries to protect my well-being when the culture of academia wanted to suck all the labor out of me and did not care what that did to my health or joy. (This has not changed, unfortunately). In my experience working with, speaking to, and teaching others about self-care, I've realized this is the situation many of us are in. While some people need help figuring out what to do for self-care, many people are already very aware of what they would do if they could manage it.

The missing piece of the self-care puzzle – why you are not doing what you think you "should" be doing – is not education. It's tapping into our core values – the stuff that is really, really important to us – and using them to leverage our self-care. It's using values to decide where our boundaries will be and how to protect them ferociously. The approach to self-care I'm going to share with you in the chapters to come is completely different than any approach you've probably seen before – and if you're like any of the people I've met in our speaking events, workshops, or research, this approach will be the missing piece you've been looking for.

Today, as I finish this book (early 2024), I feel tearful in a happy, jubilant way. I realize what I didn't when I began this book a year ago: Self-care has saved my life. Literally. I am still on my journey. I am still learning balance, but I am fighting for it ruthlessly. Self-care is part of my bones. It has opened many doors for me, including achieving this lifelong dream of writing a book. This year I have deepened my understanding of self-care and now see how it stands in protest to grind culture. I have discovered personal boundaries around my self-care at an even deeper level than before, and I know I will never stop being that person who talks about self-care constantly. I'll use my power and privilege to push back. Higher education does not need to be this way.

I hope this book empowers you to fight ruthlessly for your self-care as well (and then for everyone else's self-care). I hope you will find this book a helpful guide with ideas that make you think, "Yes! Exactly!" I hope you know I see you and know this is hard. See this book as information and support from someone who wants higher education to be a better place. And then tell me how you've changed.

In self-care solidarity,
Jorden
January 4, 2024

My Positionality (Aka Who the Heck Am I To Be Telling You Anything?)

I'm a qualitative researcher – and we're big on telling you our positionality, which is who we are and where we come from, and how that might impact what we have to say. How can you decide if anything I say is helpful or pure bunk, if you don't know who I am? Likewise, what blind spots might I have in my work because of who I am?

I'm a white settler from a small city in Southeastern Ontario, Canada, on the traditional lands of the Haudenosaunee, Anishinabewaki, Mississauga, and Wendake-NionWentsïo. I'm now a Professor at the University of Saskatchewan in Saskatoon, Saskatchewan, Canada. Saskatoon is part of Treaty 6 territory and the homeland of the Métis. I was an overachieving, perfectionistic, highly sensitive, introverted only child who loved school, learning, animals, being creative, and Lego. I am now a medium-achieving (to myself, sometimes perceived as high-achieving by others), working-against-perfectionism, highly sensitive, introverted mama who still loves all the same things. I grew up in a middle to upper-middle-class home, and my current income places me in the upper-middle class. I have a lot of sources of privilege – so much so that I forgot to note that I was white in my first draft of this section.

I grew up with social anxiety disorder and, like many kids with social anxiety, began experiencing depressive episodes as an adolescent. Growing up, I found very few places where I felt like I fit in. That feeling followed me for a long time, including into my academic career. In fact, it's probably only in the last 5–6 years that feeling has started to fade for me – around the same time I got serious about my self-care and connected with friends and colleagues who are serious about theirs. I don't think that's a coincidence.

After high school, I went to university, about 45 minutes away from home. I was a first-generation university student. I struggled at university socially and sometimes academically. My social anxiety made it nearly impossible to connect with others, and I never joined clubs or groups, or at least not in any way that lasted. My depression made it challenging to stay motivated and consistent with my academic performance. I tended to skip a lot of classes. A LOT of classes (I'm talking weeks…). However, I made some very deep connections with others – consistent with my introverted nature. With people I consider my forever ride-or-die buddies. In retrospect, I can see that my struggle with self-care began as an undergraduate. Education was everything, always. I had no balance whatsoever, and my depression and anxiety left me feeling overwhelmed constantly. Instead of taking these as signs to work on balance, I doubled down on working all the time and not looking after myself.

Six weeks into my very first semester, I decided to drop a course and needed another to fill the spot, which is how I ended up in Intro Psychology. This put me on the path to falling into being a professor and clinical psychologist. I'm not going to pretend this was a calling – my calling was to be a writer.

I was very well trained in my doctoral program. It was rigorous, thorough, and cutting-edge. The skills I learned then have served me exceptionally well in my career. But if I had to choose primary adjectives to describe my graduate school experience, they would be traumatic, chaotic, fearful, left to sink or swim (okay, that one is not an adjective), humiliating, and soul-crushing. Suffice it to say I had zero self-care skills, zero boundaries to protect myself from the grind culture of academia, and I was completely unprepared for how harsh the experience would be. I was constantly ill (probably from stress, but this is also when my chronic illness likely began), with you name it – the flu, colds, pneumonia, one extremely nasty bout of norovirus, recurring tonsillitis, strep throat – and expected to be productive throughout. One semester, with my dominant hand in a cast, I was explicitly asked why I wasn't writing more. I literally could only type with one hand.

I spent six years of my life in fight versus flight, assuming I was about to be kicked out of my program at any moment for being completely and utterly incompetent. Because I certainly received the message a lot that I was completely and utterly incompetent (as did most of my peers; we talked about this constantly). One of my most distinct memories of incompetence was running into a professor in the hallway of a building on my way to my car, being quizzed about whether the histogram bars in the SPSS printout were 100% accurate and their impatience and frustration that I didn't know. (I still don't know).

In North American clinical psychology programs, our final milestone for the Ph.D. is the completion of a year-long predoctoral residency. Creator was looking out for me because I matched with what I consider the best Canadian residency for work-life balance, at least at the time. Balance was forced on us – lovingly – by the Training Director (TD) and all my supervisors. If I worked after 4:30 pm and my TD saw me, he would tell me to go home. If I wanted to take on too many clients, my supervisor would discourage it or flat-out say no. Fridays were for seminars or professional development, and we were strongly discouraged from scheduling patients that day – and if we did, we were asked why. Some people might call this infantilizing… I call it a helpful lesson in balance. Every day from 12-1 pm, I had a lunch break with my fellow residents, where we just naturally floated our way to the cafeteria or outside to eat and catch up. My depression was more manageable. I laughed all the time. I started going to massages to destress and felt like I finally had somewhere I fit in.

That year, my biggest sources of stress were finishing my dissertation and finding a tenure-track job. I managed to do both, which is how I cried that one night in my Saskatoon apartment – where we met at the start of this book. If I had to choose adjectives to describe my first decade on the tenure track, they would be traumatic, chaotic, fearful, humiliating, and soul-crushing. Sound familiar? I'd add angrifying, sexist, and discriminatory to the list as well.

After discovering that there isn't much literature on self-care practices for those of us in higher education (or health care, helping professions, lawyers, or … pretty much anyone), I began researching self-care. Along the way, some of my students joined me. At the same time, I began a long journey (that's still ongoing) of self-care for myself.

Today, I'm in a place where I still get stressed and overwhelmed – but I know it will pass (and it does). I don't feel like I'm working all the time. And by making space for the "rest of life" in my life, I have hobbies and interests that have nothing to do with my career or role as an academic. I know what values belong to me and which are messages I receive from others but don't subscribe to. I've managed to set boundaries between myself and grind culture to protect myself, my integrity, and who I am. I've found places where I fit in, and I have had time to foster my relationship with myself, which means I don't care much about the places where I don't fit in, nor do I try to fit into them so much anymore. It also means I've learned a lot about myself: I now know I'm non-binary, which has explained a lot about my constant feelings of never quite fitting in when I was growing up. I live in a fat body and don't spend all my time ruminating about that (yes, it's possible). I understand my needs around being a highly sensitive person and how to structure my lifestyle so that my chronic illnesses (including my depression) are managed as much as possible.

For the most part, I rest when I need to, and I don't worry about "failing". If I do, it's a signal to me that my balance is off. I've learned to put people before projects, have fostered a great community of people around me, and do my best to prioritize my child over work – and I'm open about this.

This required a lot of trial and error, drawing from our research, pulling from my training as a psychotherapist, and turning a lot of current self-care advice on its head – or throwing it out altogether.

So, who the heck am I to be telling you all of this? I'm a person with a lot of lived experience with self-care. I have sources of privilege and sources of struggle. I've been in academia for 25 years. I'm a self-care researcher – and few of us are out there. I'm an expert who is still learning, and I hope I can be a teacher through this book too.

You'll hear more of my story and stories of people I've worked with throughout this book. But first, let's acknowledge how higher education is stressful to work in, what it does to our minds and bodies, the messages academia sends us, and how we can begin to push back and care for ourselves. Onward to Chapter 1!

Acknowledgments

It takes a village to overhaul your life, and it takes a village to write a book about it. I know I will accidentally exclude someone here, and I apologize profusely.

Thank you to Narelle Lemon and the team at Routledge for making this book happen. Narelle, thank you for guiding this book from a loose proposal to a finished product with enthusiastic support and kindness. Thank you to Narelle and Routledge for your flexibility through life changes, caregiving responsibilities, and multiple illnesses that led to deadline changes. Your commitment to self-care is a beautiful breath of fresh air.

Thank you to those who helped me prepare this book: Janeen Loehr, Rebekah Bennetch, and Tara Hackl, for kindly offering to review chapters and taking the time from your busy days to provide invaluable feedback and suggestions. Thank you, Arianna Gibson, for your literature review help; Kendall Deleurme for your reference and formatting help; Shawn Kauenhofen for help with figures; and Jessica Campoli, Laura Knowles, and Sarah Mohammed for your research discussed in this book. Thank you to my colleagues who got excited about the book and encouraged me to hurry up and finish it so they could read it! My heart is full with your enthusiasm and support.

Thank you to the many others who influenced my thinking about self-care and well-being, many of whom have spent hours (sometimes over years) engaged in conversations about academia, discussions of self-care, and shared resources that have helped them. Thanks for always thinking of me when you see a ridiculous corporate wellness meme in the wild. Thank you to my coaches, therapists, and my other "Team Self-Care" members. This includes Elena Ballantyne, Loleen Berdahl, Shannon Blanchet, Stryker Calvez, Alex Clark, Katie Collins, Caitlin Faas, Michelle Gagnon, Eric Denise Grollman, Sarah Hunter, Dick Katz, Katie Linder, Marla Mickleborough, Jae Morgans, P, Raul Pacheco-Vega, Steve Prime, Tim Shea, Bailey Sousa, John Paul Stephens, Cailey Strauss, Jaris Swidrovich, Douglas Tsoi, Tara Turner, Stephen Urqhart, Victoria Walton, Miranda Wells, Meagan Williams, and The Women's/Gender Non-conforming Writing Group.

Thank you to everyone who reads the Teach Me Self Care newsletter (now the Rebel Scholar Dispatch Substack), those who invited me to deliver workshops and talks, the people who asked me how my book is going, our research participants, and the Grad Students Against Burnout! (GRaB) alumni. Thank you to Queen's House for your wonderful writing space. Thank you to my "retreat tree" for keeping me company.

Thank you to the haters and the bullies. I learned from you.

Thank you to my parents, Maureen and Gene, for always supporting my career aspirations, including the dream of writing a book. You supported this process with your encouragement and, more tangibly, with the childcare, meals, and housework coverage I needed to make time to write during the last year and a half.

Last, thank you Morley. Every moment of my life has led me to you. Every day you teach me more than I could ever have learned in books about acceptance, love, play, creativity, and values. You're my favorite thing in the whole world. XO

Introduction
Stress, Burnout, and Higher Education

The work we (researchers, instructors, faculty, staff, and graduate students) do in higher education is essential. We play a critical role in the production of knowledge and the lives of others. We impact our coworkers and peers, but our mandate is also to impact students' lives. We are tasked with preparing them for the future.

In my country, Canada, there were 2.2 million post-secondary college or university students in 2020–2021 (Statistics Canada, 2022). That's a lot of lives touched by those of us who work in higher education. We do cutting-edge research that often makes the world a better place. We teach students our disciplines and skills like critical thinking, creativity, and the myriad of ways to approach problems. We attend graduate programs for a variety of reasons. Academic staff dedicate their time to helping everyone navigate and thrive in this environment. Throughout our careers, all of us will influence thousands of other people. Higher education institutions are crucial hubs for generating knowledge, innovation, and training labor (Chen & Kenney, 2007; Kitagawa, 2005; Salimzadeh, Saroyan, & Hall, 2017). Higher education experiences have lasting effects on students' lives socially (McCabe, 2016), vocationally (Bynner et al., 2003 Vaatstra & De Vries, 2007; Vermeulen & Schmidt, 2008), economically (Cunningham, n.d.), medically and psychologically (Bynner & Egerton, 2001), in terms of tolerance of diversity and equality (Bynner & Egerton, 2001; Henderson-King & Kaleta, 2016), and civic-mindedness and voting behavior (Institute for Higher Education Policy, 2005). Academic workers transform economies and lives (Johnsrud, 2008; Kitagawa, 2005). As we'll talk about in a later chapter, many people consider their academic work a calling, a passion, or a large part of their identity. Core to academia is us – the academic worker!

However, working in higher education can also be a challenge. It can cause stress and lead to burnout, negatively impacting our mental and physical health. For some of us, higher education can be a traumatizing space that does us substantial harm. As I'll talk about later in this chapter, academia sends us messages – many of them dysfunctional – about how much of our lives we should devote to it and the role of well-being, balance, and self-care in

DOI: 10.4324/9781003379805-1

higher education. But there are ways to filter through this narrative and focus on what is most important to us. There are ways to thrive in academia with balance, an emphasis on well-being, and space for self-care.

Why is Academia So Stressful?

There are many sources of stress in higher education. These stressors are well documented via a vast body of empirical inquiry, theoretical reflections, and opinion pieces. These stressors include decreasing numbers of jobs and increasing precarity of positions (Statistics Canada, 2018) (e.g., contingent, non-tenure track positions), isolation (Bozeman & Gaughan, 2011; Hawkins, Manzi, & Ojeda, 2014; Kuntz, 2012), the process of obtaining tenure (Mullen & Forbes, 2000), poor work-life balance (Hawkins et al., 2014; Ylijoki, 2013), increased workload and cuts to administrative support (Hawkins et al., 2014), time pressure (Clark & Sousa, 2018), pressure for our work to have commercial and revenue-generating applications (Allen, 2011; Demeritt, 2000), ambiguous and unclear definitions of success (Clark & Sousa, 2018), demands for soft-skills that are difficult to learn and often not taught (e.g., leading teams, resolving conflict; Clark & Sousa, 2018), sleep deprivation (Acker & Armenti, 2007), lack of collegiality and incivility/bullying (Ryan, 2012; Twale & DeLuca, 2008), long hours (Kinman, 2014), demands for both research productivity and administrative service (Gomes, Faria, & Gonçalves, 2013; Vera, Salanova, & Martin, 2010), to work more/faster and quantify one's work (Berg & Seeber, 2016; Evans, 2011; Raaper, 2016; Smith, 2000), generational differences with students (Twenge, 2009), increasing student hostility (Morrissette, 2001), consumer attitudes toward higher education (Delucchi & Korgen, 2002; Schneider, 1998), and increasing mental illness amongst students (Twenge, 2006) that we might not be trained to help with.

If you've been in academia for a while and think this problem is getting worse, you are correct: Stress levels for academic workers have increased over the past 20 years (Catano, Francis, & Haines, 2010; Gillespie, Walsh, Winefield, Dua, & Stough, 2001; Rothmann, Barkhuizen, & Tyterleigh, 2008; Watts & Robertson, 2011). Moreover, this stress is higher than in other occupations and the general population (Gillespie et al., 2001; Tytherleigh, Webb, Cooper, & Ricketts, 2005).

Many of these stressors result from administrators and governments applying neoliberal and "lean" principles to higher education, asking us to do more and more with fewer and fewer resources. For example, between 2009 and 2015, government financial support for Canadian universities reportedly declined by 1.6 billion dollars (Usher, 2018). When adopted by those "in charge" of our institutions, these values push to extract as much labor from us as possible, with as little investment as possible. For example, the application of metrics to measure our outputs (many of which won't apply across disciplines –

Figure 0.1 Academia can be a source of many stressors

Photo by Matteo Vistocco, available on Unsplash at https://unsplash.com/photos/man-holding-forehead-under-sunset-CYN6x1FyPWs

also a source of stress as we try to explain why our work is important to people who don't understand that work) along with the rise of managerialism (Spooner & McNinch, 2018), downloading of more tasks to staff combined with cuts to administrative support, and pressure for our research to have commercial applications are all examples of neoliberal values that can cause stress for higher education workers.

Higher education institutions globally are pursuing public-private financial arrangements and business-style models to increase capital (Spooner & McNinch, 2018). For example, at my institution, there has been increased pressure to create revenue-generating endeavors, and certain funding pots can only be accessed for projects that will generate a return on the institution's investment. We have also experienced a substantial loss of administrative support, which adds to the workload of those staff left behind and the faculty they support.

No matter what narrative we are told about why this is the case, I strongly believe this is a direct result of decreased government funding for higher education. Neoliberalism and the adoption of corporate values also have led to an increase in precarious (i.e., stressful!) labor such as sessional or term instructors, outsourcing services to external companies, and reducing university staff while bloating administrative positions (and salaries) (Spooner & McNinch, 2018). Reducing secure positions (and undermining the effectiveness of the faculty and staff who remain) creates a labor force that is more easily controlled, according to Noam Chomsky (Spooner & McNinch, 2018). This "cut[s] back on the possibilities of doing authentic research and serious teaching, which [from a business perspective] is an expensive waste of time" (Spooner & McNinch, 2018, p. 58).

In recent years, we have also seen an international increase in debates regarding academics' right to free speech, which is supposed to be a core purpose of tenure. Of course, with an increased reliance on precarious labor, fewer people in higher education are protected by tenure. We see some academics being fired for their criticism of systems and others using the platform of tenure to promote hate speech. Tenure itself – for those of us in the increasingly rare position of being on the tenure track – is being dismantled at many institutions, again globally (Gabriel & Dillon, 2011; Levine, 2015).

Working in academia can also bring many sources of interpersonal stress. It is no secret to many that higher education can be filled with a lack of collegiality, incivility, bullying, or outright harassment and assault (Twale & DeLuca, 2008). Recently, both internationally and locally, I've seen the rise of claims of "reverse racism" or "reverse sexism" from white male heterosexual academics who are arguably the most powerful academic workers because of their privilege. Moreover, the systems in place that are designed to address bullying, harassment, and assault are woefully inadequate – not only are they sometimes re-traumatizing for the survivors who access them, but negative career ramifications of reporting are concerningly frequent.

While I was revising this chapter, one instructor and two students were stabbed at the University of Waterloo here in Canada during a politics and gender class. The male perpetrator entered the classroom, confirmed what the topic of the class was, and assaulted them. Waterloo Regional Police confirmed this was a "planned and targeted attack". It was "a hate-motivated incident related to gender, expression, and gender identity" (Shetty, 2023).

While I was editing this book, Dr. Zijie Yan, an associate professor at the University of North Carolina, Chapel Hill, was murdered on campus by a graduate student. While defining campus shootings is complicated, there have been nine mass shootings on or near American college campuses since 1966, according to The Violence Project (Riedman & Densley, 2023). For many of us, the possibility of experiencing violence or violent death at work was not something we imagined when we began careers in higher education.

The challenges of this environment are markedly worse for minority academic workers (e.g., women, BIPOC, cultural minorities, and 2SLGBTQ+ people), particularly those from groups that hold multiple disadvantaged statuses. Such additional stressors include lack of representation (Academic Women's Association University of Alberta, 2018; Shen, 2017), particularly at higher academic ranks (Statistics Canada, 2018), lower pay (Croxford, 2018), more work in the home and less time for research (McCutcheon & Morrison, 2016), higher levels of emotional labor (Tunguz, 2016), microaggressions and overt racism (Bhattacharya, 2016; Harlow, 2003; Pittman, 2010), devaluing of scholarly contributions and the burden of representing minorities (i.e., a racial tax) (Zambrana, Wingfield, Lapeyrouse, Dávila, Hoagland, & Valdez, 2016), being viewed as having a political agenda in the classroom (Anderson & Kanner, 2011), higher rates of unwanted sexual attention (Matchen & De-Souza, 2000) and sexual harassment (Lampman, Phelps, Bancroft & Beneke, 2009; McKinney, 1990; National Academies of Sciences, Engineering, & Medicine, 2018), and biased evaluation practices (Boring, Ottoboni, & Stark, 2016; Ray, 2018; Sprague & Massoni, 2005). Mainstream academia expects that minority workers will happily co-exist with their (current and historical) oppressors (Bhattacharya, 2016) and work within oppressive institutions. This is, for example, particularly true for Indigenous academic workers in Canada who must work within a Westernized education system when that system has been the source of cultural genocide and intergenerational trauma via the residential school system (Cote-Meek, 2014).

It is critical to acknowledge that self-care is not the cure for systematic barriers and oppression in higher education, including for minority workers. As Dalia Kinsey says in her book *Decolonizing Wellness*, "[y]ou can't drink a green smoothie and cure the damage of unrelenting stress and the low-grade terror that comes with possibly being attacked, humiliated, or harmed at any moment for simply existing" (2022, p. 3). "Being silenced and simultaneously commodified or leveraged for the profit of institutions that claim to support us is a constant frustration for so many people of color" (Kinsey, 2022, p. 4)

I want to pause for a moment and share something I noticed about all this information regarding the stress of working in academia as I was gathering it together: The sources I cited represent *decades of research*. The citations I've used in this chapter were published between 1998 and 2023. I could have included some from the 1980s; I wouldn't be surprised if I could find some from even earlier. Said differently: **The stress of working in higher education is not new**. It has been documented for a long, long time. **This is known**. This information is not secret.

What to make of that? It emphasizes how these characteristics are a design feature, not a bug, for higher education. We often view all these stressful and risky experiences as a side-effect of higher education. Instead, I have come to believe that they are *purposeful, designed* features of higher education, with the primary goal of oppressing and pushing out anyone who isn't from the dominant culture (read: white, heterosexual, able-bodied men, which I will now call WHAMs). All this strife is not an inconsequential side effect of higher education. **It's how higher education is built.** As Susanna Harris notes in Pope-Ruark (2022), "If you follow the pace of academia, like flat out, if you follow what is expected of you, you are going to burnout because what is expected of you is impossible; it's almost gaslighting" (p. 120). This provides an example of what I mean by stress being a design feature of higher education.

Why is this important? Because it means **the stress we experience as part of academia is not our fault. It's academia's fault**. And academia is doing it on purpose. Can we use self-care strategies to mitigate stress? Yes. But it doesn't mean that something is wrong with us or that we are broken if we find higher education difficult or impossible to work in. The system is broken – and it was designed to be broken for most of us.

How Does this Stress Impact Us?

Prolonged stress is less than ideal for our bodies and minds. Canadian endocrinologist Hans Selye was one of the first researchers to identify what prolonged stress does to bodies in his research with rats in the 1930s. Initial stress is not so bad – our bodies respond in a healthy, adaptive way designed to provide us with the energy and physical capacity to respond to a stressor. Our HPA axis activates: the hypothalamus secretes hormones telling our pituitary gland to release the hormone ACTH. ACTH tells our adrenal glands to secrete epinephrine, norepinephrine, and cortisol. Glucose is released into the blood, and our bodies are ready to run from that giant tiger about to chase us (or answer a particularly stressful email).

However, chronic (long-term) stress is not so great for our bodies. While our body is busy getting ready to respond to the tiger or the email, increasing activity in the sympathetic division of our autonomic nervous system (ANS), it is also suppressing activity in the parasympathetic division of our ANS. As our HPA axis continues to be activated and our adrenal glands produce cortisol, our body's stress mechanism gets tired out. Eventually, this can lead to bodily states and experiences like fatigue, difficulty concentrating, and a weakened immune system (making us more likely to get colds, flu, and other viruses). Chronic stress can eventually lead to conditions ranging from burnout to heart disease to migraines. In addition, we can experience depression and anxiety, suicidality, increased illness, and risk of mortality. Stress and its consequences are related to decreased innovation and creativity (Fredrickson, 2001) and lower performance, productivity, and output (Blix et al., 1994; Danna & Griffin, 1999; Kajitani, McKenzie, & Sakata, 2016; Maslach & Leiter, 1997). All of which makes it harder to do our jobs successfully.

Specific to academia, there is, again, a substantial body of research demonstrating how hard this stress is on us. It contributes to high distress (Barkhuizen, Rothmann, & Van de Vivjer, 2014; Blix et al., 1994; Catano et al., 2010; Kinman, 2014;), psychological and physical health problems (Barkhuizen et al., 2014; Dreyer, Dreyer, & Rankin, 2010; Rothmann et al., 2008; Sang, Teo, Cooper, & Bohle, 2013), and burnout (Blix, et al., 1994; Byrne et al., 2013; Lackritz, 2004; Sabagh, Hall, & Saroyan, 2018). Burnout can be especially problematic because of its symptoms of emotional detachment and a loss of empathy for others (Alkema, Linton, & Davies, 2008; Kinman, 2014). We can experience depression and anxiety (Kataoka et al., 2014; Kinman & Jones, 2003; Shen, et al., 2014), suicidality (e.g., Dres et al., 2023), and increased illness and risk of mortality (Goh, Pfeffer, Zenios, & Rajpal, 2015). In her book, *Unraveling Faculty Burnout* Rebecca Pope-Ruark (2022) describes that her own experience of burnout included dreading going to campus, avoiding meetings, not being able to write, creating exit strategies, and feeling exhausted by students who used to be a source of professional joy for her. Being unable to empathize with or connect with students is also a red flag that I am burnt out. Pope-Ruark (2022) outlines that burnout can also lead to physical problems such as insomnia, drug and alcohol abuse, diabetes, hypertension, and pain. Unfortunately, burnout is contagious (e.g., Meredith et al., 2019).

Prolonged stress, the demands of higher education, and burnout can also be associated with unethical behavior (e.g., Salyers et al., 2015) and higher rates of questionable research practices (Banks et al., 2016; Clark & Sousa, 2018). Much of the research on this comes from medicine. For example, among medical residents, emotional exhaustion and depersonalization (both aspects of burnout) are associated with lower conscientiousness in their work (e.g., missing appointments and being late for patients; Salyers et al., 2015). Residents with higher levels of burnout also report making more medical errors (West, Huschka, Novotny et al., 2006). Regarding questionable research practices, some authors have linked pressure to publish ("publish or perish") to the likelihood of perpetrating them (Gopalakrishna, ter Riet, Vink, Stoop, Wicherts, & Bouter, 2022; Tijdink, Verbeke, & Smulders, 2014). In one study, this was the strongest predictor of questionable research practices among health professions educators (Maggio et al., 2019). Another disturbing outcome of stress and burnout in academia is that, over time, our disengagement leads to the normalization of incivility (Twale & DeLuca, 2008). As Pope-Ruark (2022) notes, academic bullying can sometimes be masked as mentoring, which means it's served with a side of gaslighting as well.

All these consequences negatively impact academia as a system too. They create associated costs for institutions and impact teaching quality and performance (Berg & Seeber, 2016). Our stress influences the stress of our students. For example, many researchers have documented how poor relationships between advisors and graduate students have been linked to graduate students' mental health concerns and academic issues (Devine & Hunter, 2017 Rummell, 2015; Tompkins et al., 2016). There are direct links between faculty well-being and performance in research and teaching. Healthy, satisfied workers can be more creative, productive, and engaged instructors and researchers. They can serve as important role models for colleagues and students, many of whom also report high levels of distress.

We can become disengaged or quit academia entirely (Zumeta & Raveling, 2001). This is academia's loss – because those who quit are more likely to be minority voices (e.g., not WHAMs); this is how higher education loses crucial diverse voices. In this way, academia continues to replicate itself as a system for the benefit of WHAMs and a site of oppression for anyone else. I'll unpack this more while discussing academia's messaging around self-care.

Academia's Messaging About Self-Care

Higher education was an early (maybe the original?) adopter of hustle culture. It's seen as normative to work long, unsustainable hours. It's seen as expected to give up all other aspects of your life to prove how dedicated you are. It's seen as heroic to ignore your physical and mental health for the good of the institution. As Pope-Ruark describes in her book, burnout is "a badge of honor" in higher education "to feel included in the cult of busyness that has cursed so many of us to fetishize productivity and reputation" (2022, p. 7). She goes on to highlight what the hustle culture of higher education expects from us:

> Our culture values external rewards and ever-escalating and often competing expectations, all wrapped in the idea that we are fortunate to be in higher education in the first place. Being seen as someone who cannot keep up or is a troublemaker could be the death knell for the career of a serious academic.... [A] reflection of how busy we can make ourselves to look important, how often we can martyr ourselves... or how much personal time and even our health we are ready to lay at the feet of the university...
>
> (p. 16)

Very few people would answer resounding yes – or even an uncertain yes – when asked if higher education is an environment that encourages self-care.

As I previously mentioned, there are decades of research on the difficulties of working in higher education and the toll it can take on our minds, bodies, and careers. Remember: This is a design feature, not a bug. **It's not you, it's academia.**

Higher education sends many messages encouraging us to *avoid* self-care rather than incorporate it into our daily habits. For example, our worth is based on our productivity, and if we cannot be successful in academia, then we are weak (Pope-Ruark, 2022). Due to adopting neoliberalism and managerialism, higher education has adopted values consistent with "the marketplace and corporate culture" (Lincoln, 2018, p. 6). This has led to adopting "coercive accountability" (Shore & Wright, 2000), where we must spend excessive time providing quantified records of what we have done and its impact – further defining our worth to the academy in terms of what we produce. As Lincoln (2018) notes, "[i]n the corporatized university, it is the amount of productivity that is audited, rather than the power or creativity or insight of that productivity" (p. 13). Thus, we must work constantly and consistently and prove our work is valuable. Our only worth is how much of the "right" stuff we produce.

This work is never done; there is always more we can do and more excellence we could bring to our performance. A 2016 survey of over twelve thousand academics reported that "academics are working for free for two extra days per week – that is, *working the equivalent of a seven-day week every week*" (Gill, 2018, p. 200; University & College Union, 2016). We receive the message that no matter how terrible our jobs are, we are lucky to have them because many qualified individuals cannot find a job in higher education (Pope-Ruark, 2022). Higher education also tells us that our "identities must revolve around our institutions and disciplines and that leaving high[er] ed[ucation] is a failure of character" (Pope-Ruark, 2022, p. 27). As we'll discuss more in Chapter 5, wrapping our identity up with our job in higher education leaves us at risk of exploitation by our employers and the academic system more generally.

Moreover, higher education culture silences us. It tells us (particularly non-WHAMs) not to speak up, complain, or share our difficulties. It tells us to hide them in shame. We can suffer alone, not realizing how many others are suffering too, because none of us feel we can share. Gill (2018) describes this odd tension between common and private: negative experiences

> were at once ordinary and everyday, yet, at the same time, they remained deeply silenced in the official and public sites of the academy. They suffused the "spaces between" - corridors, bathrooms, conference coffee breaks - but they were (and perhaps still are)[1] "officially" unrecognized, do not have "proper channels," and rarely make it onto the agendas of departmental meetings or committees or formal records of university life.

I speak from experience when I assert that pushing back against this culture and speaking up about your challenges, pain, and even your solutions (like self-care) is incredibly difficult. You might stick out like a sore thumb and be perceived as a less serious scholar or less committed to your work. However, I don't think this should stop us from pursuing self-care and well-being in higher education.

Self-Care as Resistance

As we will discuss in Chapter 6, self-care is a powerful act of resistance in higher education. To choose a life of self-care – boldly, out loud, and without apology – is to act against the extractive capitalist characteristics of higher education and to refuse to accept its culture, stress, and consequences of that stress. Higher education tells us that grinding (our soul into the ground) is the only way to succeed. This book, at its core, is all about shattering that assumption. In her book *Pleasure Activism,* adrienne marie brown writes:

> For as we begin to recognize our deepest feelings, we begin to give up, of necessity, being satisfied with suffering and self-negation, and with the numbness which so often seems like their only alternative in our society... In touch with the erotic, I become less willing to accept powerlessness, or those other supplied states of being which are not native to me, such as resignation, despair, self-effacement, depression, self-denial.
>
> (2019, p. 33).

Such "supplied states of being" are sadly common in higher education. I hope that as you develop your self-care practices (using the strategies in this book), your eyes will be opened, and you will see a new way to approach your life and work in academia. As a result, I invite you to push back against "the oppression of false peace" that is too often present in higher education. "[W]e are taught that our truths are disruptive, and that disruption is a negative act" (brown, 2017, p. 142). Our truths, to use the cliché, will instead set us free.

To me, self-care in higher education is a type of pleasure activism, which is "the work we do to reclaim our whole, happy, and satisfiable selves from the impacts, delusions, and limitations of oppression and/or supremacy" (brown, 2019, p. 13). According to brown, pleasure activism possesses the following characteristics:

- Asserts that we all need and deserve pleasure.
- Seek[s] to understand and learn from the politics and power dynamics inside of everything that makes us feel good.
- Believes that by tapping into the potential goodness in each of us, we can generate justice and liberation.

- Tapping into this potential goodness can grow a healing abundance where we have been socialized to believe only scarcity exists.
- Acts from an analysis that pleasure is a natural, safe, and liberated part of life.
- Includes work and life lived in the realms of satisfaction, joy, and erotic aliveness that bring about social and political change (p. 13).

and brown further asserts that "[u]ltimately, pleasure activism is us learning to make justice and liberation the most pleasurable experiences we can have on this planet" (2019, p. 13). In this book, self-care is the activism that will liberate us to experience pleasure in our lives and careers.

There is No One Path: Yes, It's Possible to Do Academia Differently

At this point, I'd like to introduce you to Brian. Brian is my inner Full Professor. He is an older white man with white hair, bushy white eyebrows and a bushy white beard and mustache. Brian came of age in the good old days of academia: When grants and tenure were plentiful, Brian had a secretary (and she was female, and he called her a secretary) to help him submit all his paperwork, and lecturing was the only way to teach. Brian had a stay-at-home wife who looked after everything else, leaving Brian to focus on his career.

Brian lives in my head and likes to tell me what to do. He thinks I should constantly be applying for grants and constantly writing. He does not like it when I expend energy on being a great instructor. He does not understand I have groceries to buy, laundry to do, or a child that I must make lunches for, brush the teeth of, and keep entertained and healthy.

I used to think Brian had it all right, and I needed to listen to and follow his advice. Now, I realize that Brian is a WHAM, and his advice doesn't work for me (I am not a WHAM). I've learned to externalize all those messages to Brian and stop listening to him. You might have an inner Full Professor, too – one that tells you to work constantly, that you're behind, that you're not good enough, and that you'll never make it in higher education if you don't sacrifice *everything*.

Brian (and your inner Full Professors) represent a traditional belief system about academic success. Brian epitomizes the messages that academia sends us. That there are rigid recipes for success and that anyone who deviates from them is... well, deviant! And weak, not fit for higher education, unwilling to sacrifice enough, doesn't want it bad enough... essentially doesn't deserve to be here at all.

These expectations are perpetuated by messages about fear of what will happen if you dare to disobey them. For example, any time I speak to groups of graduate students or early career researchers and encourage them to experiment with self-care, inevitably, the concern is that by doing so – and deviating from those rigid expectations – they will experience career-ending failure. Of course, no one wants to play around with trying something different when constantly fearing that disaster will absolutely occur if they do!

Sometimes these messages aren't even covert. There are lots of times in my career these messages were literal. Once, in graduate school, a clinical supervisor told me that I was an irresponsible, unethical person who would never succeed in my discipline after a family emergency led me to back out of running a therapy group.[2] (A group for which they had several other therapists, by the way).

In contrast, many people engage in self-care *and* thrive in academia. For example, well-known academic and blogger Dr. Raul Pacheco-Vega is a successful researcher, instructor, and mentor who publicly shares his experiences with pulls to overwork, rest, recovery, and self-care on his blog. In his 2014 post *On Self-Care, Balance and Overwork in Academia,* Pacheco-Vega outlines many self-care strategies. Dr. Zoë Ayres, the author of *Managing Your Mental Health During Your Ph.D.: A Survival Guide* (2022), is also an active promoter of balance and self-care in academic social media spaces.

It is possible. There are those of us out here doing it. Probably people at your very institution are doing it, but just not telling anyone (since we aren't always warmly welcomed at the faculty meetings when we boast about the 10 hours of sleep we got the night before). The good news is that if you find this niche of people, you will be supported too – they are out there, and they are amazing.

In academia, the days are short, but the years are long (the opposite of parenting). By this, I mean that while we constantly feel behind and like there is way too much work to do on any given day, our days add up to years. No one day or even a few days or, god forbid, even one month or one semester or even more will make or break your years of career success.

I encourage you to challenge this idea as a message higher education gives us to keep us in (the neoliberal, extraction capitalist) line. It's just a message; it's not truth. Brian doesn't know better; he is a creature of a different time. We don't have to prioritize his beliefs. We can tell Brian he doesn't get to make our decisions.

The truth is, as mentioned, that there is no one way to be successful in academia.[3] Academia offers a lot of different places we can focus our energies: teaching, research, service, mentoring others, community building, community-engaged scholarship and more. Yes, we have things we must do, but we also have some flexibility. Moreover, you can be productive and have a life as well.

Conclusion (TL;DR[4], But I Hope You Read)

Higher education work can be stressful. In this chapter, I identified many of those stressors and discussed how these have been around for so long that we should consider them a core feature of higher education rather than a "bug".

I outlined how prolonged stress influences our body and our mind, as well as our physical and mental health. In this chapter, we also reviewed the messages that academia sends us about self-care, and introduced the idea that self-care can be an important act of resistance. I concluded this chapter by noting that there is no "one way" to be successful in higher education.

Notes

1 I think we can say they still are.
2 Guess what, clinical supervisor? YOU were unethical in how you treated me. I don't regret my decision.
3 I cannot take sole credit for this idea. This was a hard earned conclusion I reached through my life coaching work with Dr. Caitlin Faas, coach extraordinaire.
4 TL;DR means too long; didn't read.

References

Academic Women's Association University of Alberta (2018, June 22). Equity at Canadian universities: National, disaggregated and intersectional data. https://uofaawa.wordpress.com/awa-diversity-gap-campaign/the-diversity-gap-at-canadian-universities-in-2018/

Acker, S., & Armenti, C. (2007). Sleepless in academia, *Gender & Education*, *1*, 3–24. https://doi.org/10.1080/0954025032000170309

Alkema, K., Linton, J. M., & Davies, R. (2008). A study of the relationship between self-care, compassion satisfaction, compassion fatigue, and burnout among hospice professionals, *Journal of Social Work in End-of-Life & Palliative Care*, *4*, 101–119. https://doi.org/10.1080/15524250802353934

Allen, A. (2011). The idea of a world university: Can foucauldian research offer a vision of educational futures? *Pedagogy, Culture, & Society*, *19*, 367–383. https://doi.org/10.1080/14681366.2011.607840

Anderson, K. J., & Kanner, M. (2011). Inventing a gay agenda: Students' perceptions of lesbian and gay professors, *Journal of Applied Social Psychology*, *41*, 1538–1564. https://doi.org/10.1111/j.1559-1816.2011.00757.x

Ayres, Z. (2022). *Managing your mental health during your Ph.D.: A survival guide.* Springer Nature.

Banks, G. C., O'Boyle, E. H., Pollack, J. M., White, C. D., Batchelor, J. H., Whelpley, C. E., Abston, K. A., Bennett, A. A., & Adkins, C. L. (2016). Questions about questionable research practices in the field of management: A guest commentary, *Journal of Management*, *42*, 5–20. https://doi.org/10.1177/0149206315619011

Barkhuizen, N., Rothmann, S., & van de Vivjer, F. J. R. (2014). Burnout and work engagement of academics in higher education institutions: Effects of dispositional optimism, *Stress and Health*, *30*, 322–332. https://doi.org/10.1002/smi.2520

Berg, M., & Seeber, B. K. (2016). *The slow professor: Challenging the culture of speed in the academy.* University of Toronto Press.

Bhattacharya, K. (2016). The vulnerable academic: Personal narratives and strategic de/colonizing of academic structure, *Qualitative Inquiry*, *22*, 309–321. https://doi.org/10.1177/1077800415615619

Blix, A. G., Cruis, R. J., Mitchell, B. M., & Blix, G. G. (1994). Occupational stress among university teachers, *Educational Research*, *36*, 157–169. https://doi.org/10.1080/0013188940360205

Boring, A., Ottoboni, K., & Stark, P. B. (2016). Student evaluations of teaching (mostly) do not measure teaching effectiveness, *Science Open Research*, *0*, 1–11. https://doi.org/10.14293/S2199-1006.1.SOR-EDU.AETBZC.v1

Bozeman, B., & Gaughan, M. (2011). Job satisfaction among university faculty: Individuals, work, and institutional determinants, *The Journal of Higher Education*, *82*, 154–186. https://doi.org/10.1080/00221546.2011.11779090

brown, a. m. (2017). *Emergent strategy*. AK Press.

brown, a. m. (2019). *Pleasure activism: The politics of feeling good*. AK Press.

Bynner, J. M. & Egerton, M. (2001). The wider benefits of higher education. Retrieved from: http://dera.ioe.ac.uk/5993/3/01_46_part3.pdf

Bynner, J., Dolton, P., Feinstein, L., Makepeace, G., Malmberg, L., & Woods, L. (2003). Revisiting the benefits of higher education. Retrieved January 21, 2024, from https://dera.ioe.ac.uk/id/eprint/5167/1/rd05_03.pdf

Byrne, A. C., Chughtai, A., Flood, B., Murphy, Z., & Willis, P. (2013). Burnout among accounting and finance academics in Ireland, *International Journal of Educational Management*, *27*, 127–142. https://doi.org/10.1108/09513541311297513

Catano, V., Francis, L., Haines, T., Kirpalani, H., Shannon, H., Stringer, B., & Lozanzki, L. (2010). Occupational stress in Canadian universities: A national survey, *International Journal of Stress Management*, *17*, 232–258. https://doi.org/10.1037/a0018582

Chen, K., & Kenney, M. (2007). Universities/research institutes and regional innovation systems: The case of Beijing and Shenzhen, *World Development*, *35*, 1056–1074. https://doi.org/10.1016/j.worlddev.2006.05.013

Clark, A., & Sousa, B. (2018). *How to be a happy academic*. Sage.

Cote-Meek, S. (2014). *Colonized classrooms: Racism, trauma, & resistance in postsecondary education*. Fernwood Publishing.

Croxford, R. (2018). Ethnic minority academics earn less than white colleagues. *BBC News: Family & Education*. https://www.bbc.com/news/education-46473269

Cunningham, A. (n.d.). The broader societal benefits of higher education. Solutions for our future project. Retrieved January 21, 2014, from https://docplayer.net/19989534-The-broader-societal-benefits-of-higher-education.html

Danna, K., & Griffin, R. W. (1999). Health and well-being in the workplace: A review and synthesis of the literature, *Journal of Management*, *25*, 357–384. https://doi.org/10.1016/S0149-2063(99)00006-9

Delucchi, M., & Korgen, K. (2002). We're the customer – We pay the tuition: Student consumerism among undergraduate sociology majors, *Teaching Sociology*, *30*, 100–107. https://doi.org/10.2307/3211524

Demeritt, D. (2000). The new social contract for science: Accountability, relevance, and values in US and UK science and research policy, *Antipode*, *32*, 308–329. https://doi.org/10.1111/1467-8330.00137

Devine, K., & Hunter, K. H. (2017). PhD student emotional exhaustion: The role of supportive supervision and self-presentation behaviours. *Innovations in Education and Teaching International*, *54*(4), 335–344. https://doi.org/10.1080/14703297.2016.1174143

Dres, M., Copin, M. C., Cariou, A., Mathonnet, M., Gaillard, R., Shanafelt, T., Riou, B., Darmon, M., & Azoulay, E. (2023). Job strain, burnout, and suicidal ideation in tenured university hospital faculty staff in France in 2021, *JAMA Network Open*, *6*, e233652. https://doi.org/10.1001/jamanetworkopen.2023.3652

Dreyer, S., Dreyer, L. J., & Rankin, D. M. (2010). The health and well-being of staff members at a tertiary institution in New Zealand, *ICHPER-SD Journal of Research*, 5, 45–53.

Evans, A. M. (2011). Governing student assessment: Administrative rules, silenced academics, and performing students, *Assessment & Evaluation in Higher Education*, 36, 213–223. https://doi.org/10.1080/02602930903277727

Fredrickson, B. L. (2001). The role of positive emotions in positive psychology: The broaden-and-build theory of positive emotions, *American Psychologist*, 56, 218–226. https://doi.org/10.1037/0003-066X.56.3.218

Gabriel, T., & Dillon, S. (2011, February 1). G.O.P. governors take aim at teacher tenure. *New York Times*, A1(L). Retrieved January 26, 2024, from https://link.gale.com/apps/doc/A248024595/AONE?u=anon~8bb54710&sid=googleScholar&xid=e998b5d3

Gill, R. (2018). Beyond individualism: The psychosocial life of the neoliberal university. In M. Spooner, & J. McNinch (Eds.), *Dissident knowledge in higher education* (pp. 193–216). University of Regina Press.

Gillespie, N. A., Walsh, M., Winefield, A., Dua, J., & Stough, C. (2001). Occupational stress in universities: Staff perceptions of the causes, consequences, and moderators of stress, *Work & Stress*, 15, 53–72. https://doi.org/10.1080/02678370110062449

Goh, J., Pfeffer, J., Zenios, S. A., & Rajpal, S. (2015). Workplace stressors and health outcomes: Health policy for the workplace, *Behavioral Science & Policy*, 1, 43–52. https://doi.org/10.1353/bsp.2015.0001

Gomes, A. R., Faria, S., & Gonçalves, A. M. (2013). Cognitive appraisal as a mediator in the relationship between stress and burnout, *Work & Stress*, 27, 351–367. https://doi.org/10.1080/02678373.2013.840341

Gopalakrishna, G., ter Riet, G., Vink, G., Stoop, I., Wicherts, J. M., & Bouter, L. M. (2022). Prevalence of questionable research practices, research misconduct and their potential explanatory factors: A survey among academic researchers in The Netherlands. *PLOS One*. https://doi.org/10.1371/journal.pone.0263023

Harlow, R. (2003). "Race doesn't matter, but...": The effect of race of professors' experiences and emotion management in the undergraduate college classroom, *Social Psychology Quarterly*, 66, 348–363. https://doi.org/10.2307/1519834

Hawkins, R., Manzi, M., & Ojeda, D. (2014). Lives in the making: Power, academia, and the everyday. *ACME: An International Journal for Critical Geographies*, 13, 328–351.

Henderson-King, D., & Kaleta, A. (2016). Learning about social diversity: The undergraduate experience and intergroup tolerance, *The Journal of Higher Education*, 71, 142–164. https://doi.org/10.1080/00221546.2000.11778832

Hersey, T. (2022). *Rest is resistance: A manifesto*. Little Brown Spark.

Institute for Higher Education Policy. (2005). *The investment payoff: A 50-state analysis of the public and private benefits of higher education*. IHEP. Retrieved January 26, 2024, from https://www.ihep.org/publication/the-investment-payoff-a-50-state-analysis-of-the-public-and-private-benefits-of-higher-education/

Johnsrud, L. K. (2008). Faculty work: Making our research matter more, *The Review of Higher Education*, 31, 489–504. https://doi.org/10.1353/rhe.0.0017

Kajitani, S., McKenzie, C., & Sakata, K. (2016). Use it too much and lose it? The effect of working long hours on cognitive ability. Melbourne Institute Working Paper Series. Working Paper No. 7/16. Melbourne, Australia: Melbourne Institute for Applied Economics & Social Research. Retrieved January 26, 2024, from http://dx.doi.org/10.2139/ssrn.2737742

Kataoka, M., Ozawa, K., Tomotake, M., Tanioka, T., King, B., & Lynn, C. E. (2014). Occupational stress and its related factors among university teachers in Japan, *Health*, 6, 299–305. https://doi.org/10.4236/health.2014.65043

Kinman, G. (2014). Doing more with less? Work and well-being and academics, *Somatechnics, 4*, 219–235. https://doi.org/10.3366/soma.2014.0129

Kinsey, D. K. (2022). *Decolonizing wellness*. BenBella Books, Inc.

Kinman, G., & Jones, F. (2003). "Running up the down escalator": Stressors and strains in UK academics, *Quality in Higher Education, 9*, 21–38. https://doi.org/10.1080/13538320308162

Kitagawa, F. (2005). Universities and innovation in the knowledge economy: Cases from English regions. *Higher Education Management & Policy, 16*. Retrieved January 26, 2024, from https://doi.org/10.1787/hemp-v16-art23-en.

Kuntz, A. M. (2012). Reconsidering the workplace: Faculty perceptions of their work and working environments, *Studies in Higher Education, 37*, 769–782. https://doi.org/10.1080/03075079.2010.541556

Lackritz, J. R. (2004). Exploring burnout among university faculty and incidence, performance, and demographic issues, *Teaching & Teacher Education, 20*, 713–729. https://doi.org/10.1016/j.tate.2004.07.002

Lampman, C., Phelps, A., Bancroft, S., & Beneke, M. (2009). Contrapower harassment in academia: A survey of faculty experience with student incivility, bullying, and sexual attention, *Sex Roles, 60*, 331–346. https://doi.org/10.1007/s11199-008-9560-x

LeVine, M. (2015). The dismantling of higher education. Retrieved January 21, 2024, from http://america.aljazeera.com/opinions/2015/7/the-dismantling-of-higher-education.html

Lincoln, Y. S. (2018). A dangerous accountability: Neoliberalism's veer toward accountability in higher education. In M. Spooner, & J. McNinch (Eds.), *Dissident knowledge in higher education* (pp. 3–20). University of Regina Press.

Maggio, L., Dong, T. D., Driessen, E., & Artino, A. Jr. (2019). Factors associated with scientific misconduct and questionable research practices in health professions education, *Perspectives on Medical Education, 8*, 74–82. https://doi.org/10.1007/s40037-019-0501-x

Maslach, C., & Leiter, M. P. (1997). *The truth about burnout and how organizations cause stress and what to do about it*. Jossey-Bass.

Matchen, J., & DeSouza, E. (2000). The sexual harassment of faculty members by students, *Sex Roles, 41*, 295–306. https://doi.org/10.1023/A:1023527329364

McCabe, J. M. (2016). *Connecting in college: How friendship networks matter for academic and social success*. University of Chicago Press.

McCutcheon, J. M., & Morrison, M. A. (2016). "Eight days a week": A national snapshot of academic mothers' realities in Canadian psychology departments, *Canadian Psychology, 57*, 92. https://doi.org/10.1037/cap0000049

McKinney, K. (1990). Sexual harassment of university faculty by colleagues and students, *Sex Roles, 23*, 421–438. https://doi.org/10.1007/BF00289230

Meredith, C., Schaufeli, W., Struyve, C., Vandecandelaere, M., Gielen, S., & Kyndt, E. (2019). 'Burnout contagion' among teachers: A social network approach, *Journal of Occupational and Organization Psychology, 93*, 328–352. https://doi.org/10.1111/joop.12296

Morrissette, P. J. (2001). Reducing incivility in the university/college classroom, *International Electronic Journal for Leadership in Learning, 15*, 12, Retrieved January 26, 2024, from https://journals.library.ualberta.ca/iejll/index.php/iejll/article/view/497

Mullen, C. A., & Forbes, S. A. (2000). Untenured faculty: Issues of transition, adjustment, and mentorship, *Mentoring &, Tutoring: Partnership in Learning, 8*, 31–46. https://doi.org/10.1080/713685508

National Academies of Sciences, Engineering, & Medicine. (2018). *Sexual harassment of women: Climate, culture, and consequences in academic sciences, engineering, and medicine.* Retrieved January 26, 2024, from https://www.nap.edu/catalog/24994/sexual-harassment-of-women-climate-culture-and-consequences-in-academic

Pacheco-Vega, R. (2014). *On self-care, balance and overwork in academia.* Retrieved January 21, 2024, from http://www.raulpacheco.org/2014/12/on-self-care-balance-and-overwork-in-academia/

Pittman, C. T. (2010). Race and gender oppression in the classroom: The experiences of women faculty of color with white male students, *Teaching Sociology, 38,* 183–196. https://doi.org/10.1177/0092055X10370120

Pope-Ruark, R. (2022). *Unraveling faculty burnout: Pathways to reckoning and renewal.* John Hopkins University Press.

Raaper, R. (2016). Academic perceptions of higher education assessment processes in neoliberal academia, *Critical Studies in Education, 57,* 175–190. https://doi.org/10.1080/17508487.2015.1019901

Ray, V. (2018). Is gender bias an intended feature of teaching evaluations? *Inside Higher Ed.* Retrieved January 21, 2024, from https://www.insidehighered.com/advice/2018/02/09/teaching-evaluations-are-often-used-confirm-worst-stereotypes-about-women-faculty

Riedman, D., & Densley, J. (2023, February 14). Michigan state murders: What we know about campus shootings and the gunmen who carry them out. *The Conversation.* Retrieved January 10, 2024, from https://theconversation.com/michigan-state-murders-what-we-know-about-campus-shootings-and-the-gunmen-who-carry-them-out-199912

Rothmann, S., Barkhuizen, N., & Tyterleigh, Y. M. (2008). Model of work related ill health of academic staff in a South African higher educational institution, *South African Journal of Higher Education, 22,* 404–422, Retrieved January 26, 2024, from https://hdl.handle.net/10520/EJC37437

Rummell, C. M. (2015). An exploratory study of psychology graduate student workload, health, and program satisfaction, *Professional Psychology: Research & Practice, 46,* 391–399. https://doi.org/10.1037/pro0000056

Ryan, S. (2012). "Academic zombies: A failure of resistance or a means of survival?, *Australian Universities Review, 54,* 3–11, Retrieved January 26, 2024, from https://search.informit.org/doi/10.3316/ielapa.754699476610223

Sabagh, Z., Hall, N. C., & Saroyan, A. (2018). Antecedents, correlates, and consequences of faculty burnout, *Educational Research, 60,* 131–156. https://doi.org/10.1080/00131881.2018.1461573

Salimzadeh, R., Saroyan, A., & Hall, N. C. (2017). Examining the factors impacting academics' psychological well-being: A review of research, *International Educational Research, 5,* 13–44. https://amel.net/wp-content/uploads/2024/07/salimzadeh-et-al.-2017.pdf

Salyers, M. P., Fukui, S., Rollins, A. L., Firmin, R., Gearhart, T., Noll, J. P., Williams, S., & Davis, C. J. (2015). Burnout and self-reported quality of care in community mental health, *Administration and Policy in Mental Health, 42,* 61–69. https://doi.org/10.1007/s10488-014-0544-6

Sang, X., Teo, S. T., Cooper, C. L., & Bohle, P. (2013). Modelling occupational stress and employee health and well-being in a Chinese higher education institution, *Higher Education Quarterly, 67,* 15–39. https://onlinelibrary.wiley.com/doi/10.1111/j.1468-2273.2012.00529.x

Schneider, A. (1998, Mar 27). Insubordination and intimidation signal the end of decorum in many classrooms. *The Chronicle of Higher Education.*

Shen, A. (2017). Data on number of professors and their salaries released after five-year hiatus. *University Affairs.* Retrieved January 21, 2014, from https://www.universityaffairs.ca/news/news-article/data-number-professors-salaries-released-five-year-hiatus/

Shen, X., Yang, Y. L., Wang, Y., Liu, L., Wang, S., & Wang, L. (2014). The association between occupational stress and depressive symptoms and the mediating role of psychological capital among Chinese university teachers: A cross-sectional study, *BMC Psychiatry, 14,* 329, https://doi.org/10.1186/s12888-014-0329-1

Shetty, A. (2023). "University of Waterloo stabbings a 'senseless act of hate,' police say after former student charged. CBC News. https://www.cbc.ca/news/canada/kitchener-waterloo/emergency-alert-university-waterloo-stabbing-watsafe-1.6892506#:~:text=the%20police%20update.-,%22Yesterday%2C%20Professor%20Katy%20Fulfer%20and%20two%20students%20in%20her%20Gender,Month%20is%20even%20more%20painful.%22

Shore, C., & Wright, S. (2000). Coercive accountability: The rise of audit culture in higher education. In M. Strathern (Ed.), *Audit culture: Anthropological studies in accountability, ethics and the academy* (pp. 57–89). Routledge.

Smith, N. (2000). Who rules this sausage factory? *Antipode, 32,* 330–339. https://doi.org/10.1111/1467-8330.00138

Spooner, M., & McNinch, J. (Eds.) (2018). *Dissident knowledge in higher education.* University of Regina Press.

Sprague, J., & Massoni, K. (2005). Student evaluations and gendered expectations: What we can't count can hurt us, *Sex Roles, 53,* 779–793. https://doi.org/10.1007/s11199-005-8292-4

Statistics Canada. (2018). Full-time teaching staff at Canadian universities, 2017/2018. Retrieved January 26, 2024, from https://www150.statcan.gc.ca/n1/pub/11-627-m/11-627-m2018056-eng.htm

Statistics Canada. (2022). Canadian postsecondary enrolments and graduates, 2020/2021. Retrieved January 26, 2024, from https://www150.statcan.gc.ca/n1/daily-quotidien/221122/dq221122e-eng.htm

Tijdink, J. K., Verbeke, R., & Smulders, Y. M. (2014). Publication pressure and scientific misconduct in medical scientists, *Journal of Empirical Research on Human Research Ethics, 9,* 64–71. https://doi.org/10.1177/1556264614552421

Tompkins, K. A., Brecht, K., Tucker, B., Neander, L. L., & Swift, J. K. (2016). Who matters most? The contribution of faculty, student-peers, and outside support in predicting graduate student satisfaction, *Training & Education in Professional Psychology, 10,* 102–108. https://doi.org/10.1037/tep0000115

Tunguz, S. (2016). In the eye of the beholder: Emotional labor in academia varies with tenure and gender, *Studies in Higher Education, 41,* 3–20. https://doi.org/10.1080/03075079.2014.914919

Twale, D. J., & DeLuca, B. M. (2008). *Faculty incivility.* Jossey-Bass.

Twenge, J. M. (2006). *Generation me: Why today's young Americans are more confident, assertive, entitled – Are more miserable than ever Before.* Free Press.

Twenge, J. M. (2009). Generational changes and their impact in the classroom: Teaching generation me, *Medical Education, 43,* 398–405. https://doi.org/10.1111/j.1365-2923.2009.03310.x

Tytherleigh, M., Webb, C., Cooper, C., & Ricketts, C. (2005). Occupational stress in UK higher education institutions: A comparative study of all staff categories, *Higher Education Research & Development, 24,* 41–61. https://doi.org/10.1080/0729436052000318569

University and College Union. (2016). *UCU workload survey.* Retrieved January 26, 2024, from https://www.ucu.org.uk/media/8196/Executive-summary—Workload-is-an-education-issue-UCU-workload-survey-report-2016/ucu_workloadsurvey_summary_jun16.pdf

Usher, A. (2018). The state of Canadian post-secondary education, 2018. Retrieved January 26, 2024, from https://higheredstrategy.com/the-state-of-canadian-pse-2018/

Vaatstra, R., & De Vries, R. (2007). The effect of the learning environment on compe-tences and training for the workplace according to graduates, *Higher Education*, *53*, 335–357. https://doi.org/10.1007/s10734-005-2413-4

Vera, M., Salanova, M., & Martín, B. (2010). University faculty and work-related well-being: The importance of the triple work profile, *Electronic Journal of Research in Educational Psychology*, *8*, 581–602. https://doi.org/10.25115/ejrep.v8i21.1373

Vermeulen, L., & Schmidt, H. G. (2008). Learning environment, learning process, academic outcomes and career success of university graduates, *Studies in Higher Education*, *33*, 431–451. https://www.tandfonline.com/doi/full/10.1080/03075070802211810

Watts, J., & Robertson, N. (2011). Burnout in university teaching staff: A system-atic literature review, *Educational Research*, *53*, 33–50. https://doi.org/10.1080/00131881.2011.552235

West, C. P., Huschka, M. M., Novotny, P. J., Sloan, J. A., Kolars, J. C., Habermann, T. M., & Shanafelt, T. D. (2006). Association of perceived medical errors with resident distress and empathy: A prospective longitudinal study. *JAMA*, *296*(9), 1071–1078. https://doi.org/10.1001/jama.296.9.1071

Ylijoki, O. (2013). Boundary work between work and life in the high speed university, *Studies in Higher Education*, *38*, 242–255. https://doi.org/10.1080/03075079.2011.577524

Zambrana, R. E., Wingfield, A. H., Lapeyrouse, K. M., Dávila, B. A., Hoagland, T. L., & Valdez, R. B. (2016). Blatant, subtle, and insidious: URM faculty perceptions of discriminatory practices in predominantly white Institutions, *Sociological Inquiry*, *87*, 207–232. https://doi.org/10.1111/soin.12147

Zumeta, W., & Raveling, J. S. (2001). The best and brightest for science. In M. P. Feldman & A. N. Link (Eds.), *Innovation policy in the knowledge-based economy*. Economics of Science, Technology, and Innovation (vol. 23). Springer.

Chapter 1

What Are Values and Why Should They Guide Us?

When I began my career on the tenure track, I had no idea what was important to me – other than keeping everyone happy so they hopefully[1] wouldn't fire me. I was very aware that was important to me because it created a lot of nausea-inducing anxiety that haunted me daily.

Because I didn't know what was important to me, everything became important to me. Without a compass to help me decide what to prioritize, I said yes to everything. My motivation for saying yes to everything was to show others I was a Superhero Professor Who Could Do It All (and keep them happy so they didn't fire me). I tried to be the best at everything: teaching, research, service, advising my students, housekeeping, paying off my student debt, friendship, you name it. I poured energy into creating the perfect assignments for my undergraduate classes, contributing vocally to the meetings I attended, meeting weekly (even when not needed) with my graduate students, and starting a new research program at a new institution. I spent oodles of time on self-improvement, believing I wasn't good enough as I was. I was non-discriminatory about who I spent time with, forming some unfortunately dysfunctional friendships. I excelled at nothing because I tried to be the best at everything (which is not possible). I continued my well-established pattern of burning the candle at both ends, overextending myself, and undermining my health.

For example, when my department head casually mentioned that they hadn't been able to catch me in my office, I panicked and then wholly revamped my approach to work. I began spending 9 am–5 pm (or longer) on campus, with my door wide open, to fix what I saw as a potential dealbreaker observation on their part. This choice was not only *not* in my best interest – because I work much better in the quiet at home, in track pants, with my cats – but it was nearly impossible to get anything done because my open door led to a constant stream of people entering my office to talk to me literally for hours. Hours of my day! It didn't help that my office at the time was across the hall from our department mailroom and on the way to the washroom. As a bonus, it was also around the corner from one of the largest lecture halls on campus and thus inordinately loud multiple times per day as classes switched. In short, it was (for me) a productivity nightmare.

DOI: 10.4324/9781003379805-2

So, any productivity I had been managing at home during my deep post-graduate school burnout immediately went up in smoke as I tried to work in a context that was unworkable for me. Just because one person made what was undoubtedly an offhand, meaningless comment to me. In contrast, if I had been able to set boundaries appropriately, based on my values and my knowledge of what works best for me, I would have asked my department head if they wanted to set up a time to grab coffee and chat, and continued working partially at home where I was comfortable, felt safe, and was productive.[2]

Know Yourself: What Are Core Personal Values?

As you can probably see from my story, understanding what's important to us (i.e., our core values) is a critical base for effective self-care. Without understanding our values and the contexts that are best for us, we have no compass to help us decide what direction to move in. We have no algorithm to help us decide how to spend our time, when to set, and where to place boundaries. And without the ability to sort through opportunities, we might just go with the flow and pursue all of them, like I did in my first years of the tenure track.

"Core personal values" is a phrase you might have encountered before, as it is gaining traction and value (see what I did there?), particularly within self-help literature. People are using core values as the base for all kinds of work we can do on and for ourselves. This is good because values are important, so let's celebrate more people hearing about them! Unfortunately, it also means that there are lots of definitions of values floating around out there, and they might be watered down compared to the lingo we use within the empirical psychological literature on values and human change. In the remainder of this chapter, we will discuss what values are and why knowing our values is crucial for approaching our self-care. In the next chapter, we'll work on helping you identify YOUR core personal values.

Core personal values, at their broadest level, represent what is most important to us, what we stand for, and the characteristics we want to be known for. I use the term "core values" to mean those that are really, really critical to you in this season of your life. Your "ride or die" values. The ones that are painful not to live by. **Core values are our why.**

I adopt Steven Hayes' definition of values from Acceptance & Commitment Therapy (ACT, pronounced as one word): "Values are chosen qualities of purposive action (i.e., being and doing) that can never be obtained as an object, but can be instantiated moment by moment" (Hayes, n.d.). In this model, verbs and adverbs are often used to express values.

Let's unpack that definition a little bit further, slowly. First, values are chosen[3] by you. That is, **no one can assign or tell you your values** (although they will undoubtedly try). When it comes to values, you're the boss, applesauce.[4] Just like people are different, we all hold different values. If you look around you professionally, you can probably identify people you work with who hold different values. Some people in higher education are very committed to teaching, and some consider it a chore they wish they could escape. While some people do nothing but community-based scholarship, others prefer to stay in the lab. Lots of people employed in higher education want it to be fairer, more equitable, and provide safer spaces. Other people don't see any problems. Some staff answer emails at all times of the day. Others strictly work their shift and then focus on the rest of their lives. All these choices are grand, as long as they work for the person choosing them.

Pursuing a life consistent with our values is critical for thriving. A life disconnected from our values will feel bland, monotonous, and sometimes unfulfilling and painful. I recently dug out my notes from an Effective Academic workshop facilitated by Bailey Sousa and Alex Clark (authors of *How to Be A Happy Academic*). I found scrawled and underlined across the top of my notes: "Checking your values at the door when you join academia is going to make you miserable". It certainly made me miserable, as I shared with you in that story about my very first semester as an assistant professor.

Likewise, living a life focused on someone else's values will feel stressful, soul-sucking, and potentially meaningless. When you hear stories of people pursuing specific degrees or disciplines because other people in their lives want them to, that's an example of pursuing someone else's values. And while we might succeed at that endeavor, it will never feel as rewarding or joyful as succeeding in ways that match our values. A key question from ACT that can help you distinguish between your values and someone else's is this: If I could pursue this [thing] but not tell anyone about it, would I still do it? If the answer is no, you might be pursuing a value that is not yours. When we pursue what is important to us, we will feel motivated and pulled to do it, even if we do it quietly, without announcing it. (But hey, it also feels fantastic to share our joyous, value-consistent pursuits with people who love us and will be happy for us, so I hope you have or can foster relationships where you do so).

Without values, we have no compass. We flail around like fish unceremoniously hauled from the lake into a boat – not knowing which direction to go, not sure what to do, but knowing **this is definitely not it if I'm going to survive.** When I tried to succeed at everything that was me flailing around. And that lifestyle was not survivable for me.

Second, Hayes describes values as "purposive action (i.e., being and doing)". This means that while values are cognitive concepts in our minds, they are useless without accompanying being and doing (i.e., actions) consistent with those values. Thinking about our values is not enough. We must also live our lives – in our choices and behaviors – aligned with those values. This is what Hayes means when he says we can "instantiate [them] moment by moment". In as many moments of our lives as possible, we can choose to act, behave, and live consistently with our values, even when it's difficult or not necessarily enjoyable.

For example, my child and I unwind after school and work with some screen time. We need some quiet time to recharge after our busy days. One day last week, I wanted to spend my screen time on my laptop finishing an episode of a television show that has sucked me in. My kiddo was watching a video on our shared iPad about their favorite video game, and they really wanted me to watch it too. After one or two interruptions of my television show, I closed my laptop. I suggested we sit on the couch together and watch the video – because being a present parent who supports secure attachment is a core value of mine. Did I feel joy about ending what I actually wanted to do, to watch a video about a game I admittedly don't understand? Not really. Did I do it anyway because it was consistent with my values? Yes. And my kiddo loved every moment of using that video to teach me about the game they love.

While **it's great to know our values, we must also align our behavior with them**. This alignment, within ACT, is known as valued living (Hayes, Strosahl, & Wilson, 2012). While we won't be perfect at valued living 24/7 (there are days I choose my television show!), we want to strive toward valued living as much as possible. If someone followed you around for a few days, observing your behaviors, would they be able to figure out what some of your core values are? If yes, your actions align well with your values, and you are higher in valued living. If not, you are lower in valued living, and might want to consider choosing different actions or behaviors that better align your values and life with one another.

Understanding our values and being motivated toward valued living provides critical information for choosing what to do with our time and actions, especially if we are presented with many options. For example, let's discuss a (surprisingly) controversial academic topic: out-of-the-office email autoreplies. If I had to think of my number one academic activity that epitomizes the (often ineffective, but always soul-crushing) grind culture of academia, it's email.[5] It's hard to imagine that when email was first introduced into higher education, it was claimed it would make our lives easier (and let's be honest, we believed it). To me, email is (mostly) a never-ending task that sucks our attention in non-intentional ways and keeps a lot of us from doing the work that is most important in our careers. (You can probably tell I have intense feelings about email.)

I adore out-of-the-office email autoreplies and use them liberally. I use them when I'm on vacation or leave, but I also use them for particularly busy times at work when I know I won't get to my email regularly or promptly. I have several core personal values that lead me to prioritize time off from my email. As I'll discuss more later, one of my core values is "Creating Beautiful Things". Too much email can interfere with my ability to move toward that value. For example, I've noticed a difference in my ability to show up to write this book (a beautiful creation) on days when I keep my email open versus days when I close it. If I spend my energy on email, the trade-off is that I have less energy for creative pursuits. Email and creative pursuits are morally neutral choices; choosing either would be fine. If I want to be productive on this book, however, I should not choose to spend excessive time on email. Moreover, the book is more values-aligned for me than many of the emails I receive.

There is a considerable problem with out-of-the-office autoreplies: Most people do not believe you when you use them. This is why we slap on an autoreply but still receive emails that say something like this: "Hey, I know you have an autoreply that says you're on vacation, but…." or "I understand you're off right now, but this is urgent", or emails that don't even attempt to apologize for ignoring our auto-replies and expect us to reply anyway. A colleague at a coffee shop once approached me while I was on vacation and relayed to me that a bunch of people were upset with me because I was not replying to emails about scheduling a meeting when I was on vacation even though I had an autoreply saying that I wouldn't be. I had no idea because I wasn't checking email … just like my autoreply said. I had also (I thought) pre-empted this problem by telling everyone my availability for the meeting before my vacation started. This was a critical lesson for me in my early working days in higher education: No one believed my autoreply.

Why do we not believe most people's out-of-the-office autoreplies? **Because so many people send us emails anyway when they are out of the office despite an autoreply saying they won't.** I know many people whose values seem very consistent with taking time off. Staff, graduate students, and professors who value time with their family, rest, travel, and all kinds of other things that should lead to taking time off (completely off). I also consistently know many of those people will email me back, even when they are on vacation. Tricia Hersey, Nap Minister, and author of *Rest is Resistance* describes academia as the birthplace of grind culture (Hersey, 2022). Part of the grind is feeling compelled to always be available. To override values and related behavior and send emails anyway. This is an excellent example of values-inconsistent behavior (or acting low in valued living).[6]

Not only does values-inconsistent behavior often feel … well, gross (answering emails from the beach when you said you promised yourself you wouldn't even look at email is not a fun feeling … and I know this from experience), but it's likely to lead to dissatisfaction and burnout too. As Sarah Odell describes in her book *Saving Time*,

> …I doubt burnout has ever been solely about not having enough hours in the day. What first appears to be a wish for more time may turn out to be just one part of a simple, yet vast, desire for autonomy, meaning, and purpose.
>
> (Odell, 2023, p. xv).

We pursue meaning and purpose by knowing our values and valued living (i.e., aligning our behaviors with those values). Doing so is indeed protective against burnout, as Odell speculated.

The Difference Between Values & Goals

Hayes' definition describes values as something "that can never be obtained as an object" (n.d.). We cannot "accomplish" our values – they are never finished. This is how values are different from goals. For example, one of my core personal values is something I have labeled "Richness of Life". I cannot put "have richness of life" on a to do list and cross it off. Likewise, "be a present parent who promotes secure attachment" will never be work I'm done with. I will pursue it forever; it is not something I will ever obtain and stop working toward.

Things that we *can* accomplish or check off a list are goals. Whereas values can never be accomplished, goals can. Goals are actions we can cross off a list when they are achieved. Goals can be – and absolutely should be – linked to values. For example, you might value "being a loving and responsible pet owner" if you have pets. This is not something you can cross off a to-do list about having a pet. But you might strive toward this value with a goal of "Take Fido to the vet every year". One (the goal of annual vet visits) can be accomplished, but the other (wanting to be a responsible pet owner) is never fully finished. "Can I check this off a to-do list?" is the magic question for telling the difference between values and goals. Figure 1 summarizes these differences.

To return to my ~~rant~~ observation about not respecting our own or others' out-of-office autoreplies: We might decide to write an autoreply for any number of values (e.g., prioritizing rest or traveling somewhere new), but our goals (i.e., behaviors) are to: (1) write and set up an autoreply and (2) follow through by not emailing anyone while we are away. Those goals can be accomplished and crossed off a list, even if "prioritizing rest" is a value we pursue for a lifetime. The behavior of following through with those goals is called committed action. Committed action is essential for valued living.

Remember, your values will not be the same as my values. I'm not saying you're no longer allowed to check your email from vacation – you're the boss of your own time off, applesauce. If you want to check your emails and even reply to all of them, you can do so! My example is here to illustrate values, valued living, and goals. You can substitute examples that work for you (and there will be many more examples as we move forward together).

Values	Goals
never, ever finished	can be accomplished
cannot check off my to-do list	can check off my to-do list

Figure 1.1 Values vs. goals

Ideally, our values lead to our goals, which inform our behavior. In the context of this book, we will use our values to develop self-care goals and behaviors, as well as work boundaries to support our self-care. But all these linked concepts can be applied to any component of your life that you wish.[7]

How Exactly Are Values Helpful?

As I mentioned, values can provide a compass for us to know what direction we want to move in with our behavior and actions. Values can also provide an important filter through which we can make decisions. Last, values can lead us to know what boundaries to set (with ourselves and others) to protect our well-being.

Just as a compass will always point due North, so we can use it to decide which direction we want to head in, our values provide us with information about what direction to take our behavior in (and what direction *not* to go in). For example, suppose Fido eats a dead animal when we take him to the dog park and subsequently can't stop vomiting. In that case, we can use our value of "being a responsible pet owner" to point us in the direction of making a call or an appointment with the vet to get Fido checked out. If we, instead, chose to ignore Fido's vomiting until he just got sicker and sicker, that would be us choosing to move in a direction *away* from our value of being a responsible pet owner. Calling the vet is a committed action (Hayes et al., 2012) high in valued living. Not calling the vet is an action low in valued living. And while we can't check the value of "being a responsible pet owner" off, we can check off our goal of "call the vet".[8]

Values are also useful as decision-making tools. Since I know that being a "present parent who promotes secure attachment" is a core value for me, it means that I end work at 3 pm every weekday to pick my kiddo up from school to spend a bit of time decompressing together and being present with one another before our evening activities, chores, or responsibilities begin. This helps me decide to say no to meetings held after 3 pm,[9] and I use this timeframe to structure my workday.

You can also imagine values as a decision-making flow chart or filter through which we can decide how to expend our time and effort. In his 2011 paper on leadership for learning, Philip Halinger describes a concept I love called values leadership. Halinger notes that "[v]alues define both the ends towards which leaders will aspire as well as the desirable means by which they will work to achieve them" (p. 128). In this quote, you can think of the ends toward which leaders aspire as being values, and the desirable means being our goals or committed actions. In other words, values define what we aspire to and help us set our goals (means) by which we will work on those aspirations. And if you think, "I'm not a leader …" think again – in higher education, we are all leaders in some form. People always observe and learn from us. Remember when I described those people I know who will email me even when they are on vacation? I learned that they don't adhere to their autoreplies. We will discuss how we influence others, particularly regarding self-care, in Chapter 6.

We can also use our values as "substitutes for information" (Leithwood & Stager, 1989) when making decisions in ambiguous or low-information contexts. That is, when uncertain of what to do, we can plug into our values to help decide what action to take. Remember my description of my first semester on the tenure track and how, by being unable to clarify what was important to me, I just tried to excel at everything? If I'd been able to fall back on my values, I could have used them to guide me in that seemingly ambiguous situation where everything felt equally important. I probably would have spent more time getting my research off the ground than trying to write the perfect assignment for my undergraduates. (Spoiler alert: The perfect assignment doesn't exist anyway).

Using values to define our aspirations can help us evaluate possible actions. For example, let's say a colleague approaches you and wants you to join a committee that is important to them, and they think you'd be great for. Do you do it? You might want to check if it fits with your values. There are a lot of values that might help with this decision – the value of your relations with your colleagues, how important the topic of the committee is to you, what you might need to sacrifice to have time for the committee and if the sacrifice will be worth it … All of these are personal values – you can probably see (again) how there are no right or wrong answers when we use our values to help us make decisions. Halinger might ask, "Would participating in this committee move me closer to what I aspire to? Or distract me/interfere with what I aspire to?" If I'm on a committee aligned with my values, I will bring 110% to that work. If I choose one that causes me too much stress or emotional harm or is not aligned with what I consider important (i.e., my values), it could be the world's easiest committee, and I would still be a terrible fit for that work. Additionally, because I pick my child up from school every weekday, I couldn't be on a committee that gathers at 4:30 pm for every meeting.[10]

Last, values can tell us where to set boundaries to protect our self-care and well-being. What happens when I read someone's autoreply and never receive a reply while they are out of the office? They set a boundary for me (and anyone else sending them an email), and I learned they meant it. If you didn't care about protecting your vacation time (which is completely fine), you probably wouldn't bother to set up that autoreply (boundary) in the first place (which is also completely fine).

If we don't have a compass (values) and accompanying goals and actions, we can easily find ourselves swept along in the strong current of higher education work. We will just be doing, doing, and doing without any overarching framework to help us decide what to do (and why). We can spend time and energy working hard but not accomplishing what matters. Even if you are in a position where your job role is very clearly defined, values can often inform

Figure 1.2 Understanding what is important to us helps guide us

Photo by Ian Schneider, available on Unsplash at https://unsplash.com/photos/two-person-standing-on-gray-tile-paving-TamMbr4okv4

how you structure some of your work (or your approach to work). For example, after the onset of the COVID-19 pandemic, I know many staff at my institution who applied for and received approval to work remotely for part (or sometimes all) of their work. Generally, they asked to do so because it aligned with their values.[11]

If we don't make plans for our well-being and careers, we will be easily caught up in other people's plans – and other people won't always (or rarely) have YOUR best interest at the heart of those plans. This can happen especially early on in our careers or in precarious employment situations. There are so many people who can influence our careers that we might spend more time trying to make them happy than being able to reflect on, let alone live, our values. (Like me trying to force myself to be productive in my on-campus office while legions of colleagues stopped by to say hi on their way to get their mail. I enjoyed getting to know them and needed to finish my work, so I should have found a compromise that worked for me). As we'll talk about in later chapters, knowing our values – even when we feel like we might not be able to live our lives consistently in line with them – is still an essential source of information.

Again, it's important to note that there are no right or wrong values, committed actions, or ways to engage in valued living. Between the number of potential core values and the combinations in which any human being could hold them, the odds of two people's core values being exactly the same are very low. **Values and behaviors are morally neutral.** That message is so important we're going to return to it repeatedly, and I'm going to repeat it right now: Values and behaviors are morally neutral. Read it as many times as you need to. Stick it on a post-it note at your desk or bathroom mirror. There are no right or wrong behaviors. (Even that behavior you're thinking of right now, nope, that's not wrong either).

What matters is whether our actions are workable for us in the context of our actual lives. There are a million ways to be productive, set up an email autoreply, be a responsible pet owner, and be a present parent who promotes secure attachment. And all of them are excellent ways. In other words, again: You're the boss.[12]

Stacking The Deck: Self-Determination Theory & Valued Living

Something fantastic happens when we align our behavior and actions with our values. It feels good! It feels good emotionally, in our bodies and our hearts. It feels right and grounded and just lovely.

When we choose behaviors that we want to do and are aligned with our values (i.e., committed actions toward valued living) we get more out of them! Social psychologists refer to these types of motivators as "intrinsic motivation". We don't need someone to reward us or pay us to want to do those things we feel intrinsically motivated by. We will find time for them, find them more rewarding, get more positive emotions out of them, and feel good about doing them – all consistent with self-determination theory.

"Self-determination theory assumes that the human organism is evolved to be inherently active, intrinsically motivated, and oriented toward developing naturally through integrative processes. These qualities need not be learned; they are inherent in human nature" (Deci & Ryan, 2011, p. 417). According to self-determination theory, we can get a lot of satisfaction from behavior that meets three basic needs: competence, autonomy, and relatedness. Moreover, self-determination theory tells us that pursuing extrinsically motivated goals (i.e., the ones we do because other people will judge us otherwise or those we do only because we'll get paid to do them) can be associated with negative outcomes.

> Strongly pursuing extrinsic life goals, whether because of an individual difference or a prompt, has led to less wellbeing, more ill-being, and poorer performance, presumably because the extrinsic aspirations do not directly satisfy the basic needs, and indeed often crowd out or compromise their satisfaction.
>
> (Deci & Ryan, 2011, p. 424).

For example, if we begin to pay people to do something they were previously intrinsically motivated to do, they will lose interest in it – this is called the overjustification effect (The Decision Lab, n.d.).

Using our core personal values and self-determination theory to approach our work and self-care practices allows us to "stack the deck" in our favor. They help us develop self-care plans that we want to engage in, making it easier to find the motivation to create time and space for ourselves and craft what psychologists call a "life worth living". In other words, engaging in actions aligned with our values is much easier than not. Let's capitalize on this to make our self-care actions (and work decisions that support our self-care) as easy as possible.

Side note. In my experience, we can sometimes get suspicious of things that seem easy. Grind culture (the "collaboration of capitalism and white supremacy"; Hersey, 2022, p. 12) says that life must be constant work, that you are a machine that can optimize your productivity with the right inputs to get the "correct" outputs and that your sole purpose in life is to produce (labor, to generate wealth for others). When something is easy, it can feel so unusual compared to grinding that we can suspect we aren't working hard enough, feel like we're being selfish for choosing something easy, or believe it's only easy because we aren't pushing ourselves enough. Grind culture tells us that we must earn self-care, rest, and joy but simultaneously sends the message that we have never done enough or produced enough to have earned them. Thus, if we engage in self-care before we have "earned it", we are somehow being lazy, irresponsible, or breaking the rules. I am here to tell you that it is a powerful act of resistance to try to make your life easier. By doing so, you are pushing back against all those dysfunctional messages discussed in the Introduction that higher education gives us about self-care. Making my life easier – especially as someone with chronic illness – underlies many of my self-care choices. We'll talk about this more in later chapters too.

Let's consider the start of a new year as an example of self-determination theory in action. For many people (but not all), January 1st is celebrated as the start of a new calendar year. What do many people do to celebrate the start of a new year? They set resolutions! Maybe you have set resolutions before (I know I have).[13] For many, these resolutions do not stick – for example, gyms might be packed in January but empty in February. We might get the tools for a new hobby, and they might quickly gather dust in a corner. I often ask for new appliances for Christmas that I believe will be life-changing, and then it's March (or later) before I unbox them.[14]

Part of the reason that our resolutions might fail is that they weren't values-consistent, workable choices guided by self-determination theory to begin with. In other words, as I often say to my clients: "Maybe you haven't followed through on that [behavior] because you genuinely don't want to do it!".

This is especially true for any resolutions we make from a place of "should" (aka punishment) like "I should lose weight", "I should exercise more because

I'm out of shape", or "I should start cooking more because the other moms are judging my kid's highly processed lunch".[15] Remember, working toward something due to fear of what might happen otherwise is not motivating. It's instead trying to do something out of shame and that can be very demoralizing.

It's hard enough to start a new behavior (or quit an old behavior) cold turkey. It's even harder to do it when we don't have a reason to be doing it, aren't intrinsically motivated, or don't even want to do it. I could set so many New Year's resolutions that I know I would never, ever even start because I don't want to do them, nor do I have a (values-consistent) reason to compel me to do them. Again, because grind culture spends a lot of time telling us what we "should" do (and that our lives should be hard and focused only on what we produce), this might be a much more revolutionary idea than it should be.

Conclusion (TL;DR, But I Hope You Read)

In this chapter, I shared my story of feeling lost and overcommitted in my early years on the tenure track because I was not using values to guide my decisions. We discussed a definition of values and unpacked its characteristics. I introduced the concept of valued living and used the example of email autoreplies to illustrate it (and provide an example of how you can do something differently in academia to make it workable for you). Values are not goals, so we differentiated between them. Last, we talked about how values can help us and how using self-determination theory allows us to stack the deck in our favor when it comes to valued living, especially making time for self-care actions. Now it's time to identify YOUR values.

Notes

1 Sadly, I wasn't entirely convinced even keeping everyone happy would prevent me getting fired, which I now recognize as a raging case of imposter syndrome too.
2 We see this playing out similarly now "post"-pandemic, with many workers discovering that they are happier and more productive while working remotely but some employers dictating they return to the office or other colleagues misinterpreting this preference for "disengagement" or "laziness". This is an example of how higher education can set up the message of "one way" to do things and shame anything that deviates from that "one way". Despite the evidence supporting the effectiveness of remote work.
3 While Hayes says values are chosen, I personally suspect that our core personal values are even deeper than that, and that it can be very difficult to explain why a particular value is important to you. That is, they become, in my opinion, an inherent part of who we are.
4 Get ready to hear this a lot.
5 For those of you better able to tolerate or even enjoy email, please tell me your secrets.
6 Please, fight back. Put your autoreply on and follow through on it. Even better, let your autoreply say that you will not be responding to any emails received while you are away, and that people will have to email you again and then delete them all

when you get back. I promise if it's important someone will email you again. Resist the grind!

7 All these concepts are used in ACT, an evidence-based psychotherapy that can be used to treat various presenting concerns.

8 This is a great example of how valued living doesn't always feel pleasant. I am never excited about an unexpected vet bill, and I doubt you are either.

9 I acknowledge that the power and privilege of being tenured and promoted makes this decision a lot easier for me. I doubt I would have been able to make such a decision before this career stage, and not everyone will have the power and autonomy to make this specific decision.

10 And this is how we end up with a lack of representation on committees, in this example, a lack of representation of voices of those who have caregiving responsibilities in addition to their careers. But as we will discuss later, you don't have to sacrifice your well-being to attempt to change a system.

11 It is important to acknowledge that there are, however, many staff, students, and faculty who are not receiving the accommodations they need to do their best work and be their best selves. For example, those who are requesting hybrid options for work and are being denied for no clear reason other than someone else's preference for being in-person. As someone with a chronic illness, I find this ableist and discriminatory.

12 Personally, however, I would prefer that you refrain from behaviors that actively hurt others.

13 Reminder: setting resolutions or not, what those resolutions might be, and following or not following those resolutions are all morally neutral choices.

14 I'm looking at you, homemade ice cream maker that hasn't been used yet.

15 How would another mom know what's in my kid's lunch, you might ask? I don't know, but it still haunts me.

References

Clark, A., & Sousa, B. (2018). *How to be a happy academic: A guide to being effective in research, writing, and teaching*. Sage.

Deci, E. L., & Ryan, R. M. (2011). Self-determination theory. In P. A. M. Van Lange, A. W. Kruglanksi, & E. T. Higgins (Eds.), *Handbook of theories of social psychology* (pp. 416–437). Sage.

Halinger, P. (2011). Leadership for learning: Lessons from 40 years of empirical research. *Journal of Educational Administration, 49*(2), 125–142. https://doi.org/10.1108/09578231111116699

Hayes, S. C. (n.d.). The six core processes of ACT. Retrieved January 26, 2024, from https://contextualscience.org/the_six_core_processes_of_act

Hayes, S. C., Strosahl, K. D., & Wilson, K. G. (2012). *Acceptance and commitment therapy* (2nd ed.). Guilford.

Hersey, T. (2022). *Rest is resistance: A manifesto*. Little Brown Spark.

Leithwood, K. A., & Stager, M. (1989). Expertise in principals' problem solving. *Educational Administration Quarterly, 25*(2), 126–161. https://doi.org/10.1177/0013161X89025002003

Odell, J. (2023). *Saving time: Discovering a life beyond the clock*. Random House.

The Decision Lab. (n.d.). Why do we lose interest in an activity after we are rewarded for it? The overjustification effect, explained. Retrieved January 26, 2024, from https://thedecisionlab.com/biases/overjustification-effect

Chapter 2

Identifying Your Core Values

Now that we've discussed values and how to use them to set the stage for effective self-care, we must figure out our core values. Knowing what drives us helps us live our lives in ways that make us feel rewarded, connected, and alive. Usually, when we approach this moment in workshops and talks I deliver, I receive one of three reactions:

1 Sounds awesome. Let's freaking do it!
2 I already know my values, and this is a waste of time.
3 Holy crap, how can I not know what my values are? Who am I even??

For those in category #1, you can skip ahead until I tell you to resume reading. Read on for those in category #2 or #3.

If you already know some of your core values, that's fantastic. You are ahead of the game! Moreover, you have spent some time considering what's important to you, and that can be hard to find time for and a challenging area of our psyche to explore. In my experience working with clients using Acceptance & Commitment Therapy (ACT) and people attending our self-care workshops, regularly revisiting values identification work can still be helpful. While I don't believe our actual values change frequently throughout our lives, it is undoubtedly the case that as the seasons of our lives shift, we might define our values slightly differently or decide to prioritize different values than we have previously. We'll talk more about this later. I encourage you to consider completing the exercises in this chapter, even if you understand your values well. You might find some surprises!

Sometimes, we also assume our values without critically evaluating if they genuinely come from inside us or if they are ones we feel obligated to see as important. Again, we are all swimming in the same water of grind culture, which sends us very specific messages about what we should value (e.g., money, buying things, being productive, self-improvement) and what we should not (e.g., rest, slowness, daydreaming, imagination, hobbies we do just for the hell of it). Academia can be relentlessly strong with its messaging about what

DOI: 10.4324/9781003379805-3

is important. It is easy to be socialized in higher education to accept those messages without critically evaluating if they work for us.

In addition, those of us working in higher education tend to skew toward being the overachieving types. You might assume that achieving is one of your values just by working in higher education (Spoiler Alert: It might not be). The reality, however, is that people pursue any career for many different reasons. Many of us involved in higher education have been swept up in a river of its values, finding ourselves carried downstream while trying to resist the current. Or we're so busy and tired that we have never had time to think about what we value. This is an opportunity to take that time.

For anyone who might be freaking out because you don't already know what your values are: That's okay. In higher education, we are rarely, if ever, encouraged to slow down and reflect on anything, let alone what's important to us as unique human beings. Again, grind culture is busy telling us to produce – we are expected to excel at everything and do all our work tasks perfectly. As an oppressive, extractive capitalist system, it is in higher education's best interest for us never to slow down and ask, "Hey, what do I want here?" For some of us, working in higher education has also involved a lot of personal sacrifices such as frequent moving, precarious labor, postponing other primary life goals, and living at a distance from our families. When we are too busy doing all of that, of course we aren't going to spend time reflecting on what our values are. That's okay.

Note to those in category #1: You can resume reading here.

Alright, starting from a (semi-)blank slate – let's figure out your values.

Deductive & Inductive Methods for Identifying Core Values

There are two general ways to identify our core values: Deductive and inductive methods. Deductive methods work in a top-down fashion. They show us existing conceptualizations of core values, and we evaluate those values for "fit" with ourselves. They give us a menu of potential values to choose from. Inductive methods, in contrast, are bottom-up. We use our observations and information about ourselves to generate an understanding of our values and which ones we want to prioritize in any given season of our lives, which, as I mentioned, we will discuss more later.

Neither approach is better than the other – both have advantages and disadvantages. They work nicely as a complement to one another. I've worked with clients and workshop groups who uncovered different core values using each method. Combining them gives us a more complete picture of those values. I will explain both approaches, discuss their pros and cons, and share some examples.

One of the most well-known ways for deductively identifying values in ACT is a self-report measure called the Valued Living Questionnaire

(Wilson & DuFrene, 2009). The Valued Living Questionnaire has two steps: (1) Identifying which suggested values feel essential to you, and (2) rating how high or low you might be based on how much your life reflects those values right now (i.e., valued living). There are no right or wrong answers on the Valued Living Questionnaire. Here is the Valued Living Questionnaire so you can take it:

Below are some domains of life that are valued by some people. We are concerned with your subjective experience of your quality of life in each of these domains. One aspect of quality of life involves the importance one puts on the different domains of living. Rate the importance of each domain on a scale of 1 to 10; 1 means that the domain is not at all important, and 10 means that the domain is very important. Not everyone will value all of these domains, or value all domains the same. Rate each domain according to **your own personal sense of importance.**

 1 Family relations (other than marriage or parenting)
 2 Marriage/couples/intimate relations
 3 Parenting
 4 Friendships/social relations
 5 Employment
 6 Education/training
 7 Recreation
 8 Spirituality
 9 Citizenship/community life
10 Physical well-being

In this section, we would like you to give a rating of how **consistent** your actions are with each value. Everyone does better in some domains than others. We are NOT asking about your ideal in each domain. We want to know how you think you have been doing **during the past week.** Rate each item on a scale of 1 to 10; 1 means that your actions have been fully inconsistent with your value, and 10 means that your actions have been fully consistent with your value.

 1 Family relations (other than marriage or parenting)
 2 Marriage/couples/intimate relations
 3 Parenting
 4 Friendship/social relations
 5 Employment
 6 Education/training
 7 Recreation
 8 Spirituality
 9 Citizenship/community life
10 Physical well-being

As you can see, the Valued Living Questionnaire gives you a list of possible values that you might or might not find important. It then asks you to rate how consistent your behavior has been with your valued domains. Remember, whatever you value (or don't value) is perfectly okay – just like people are different, their values are different too. There are no right or wrong values to hold. Plus, values and behaviors are morally neutral. You are allowed to hold whatever values you have. And if you're in a place where you feel like you need permission for that (because it's hard sometimes), then please know that I am giving it.

A considerable advantage of deductive approaches to identifying values is that they give us a place to start. When asked, "What are your core personal values?" sometimes people don't even know where to begin. Using a list, like the Valued Living Questionnaire, can give us a place to start with some suggested values. However, having a template can sometimes be limiting. It can also activate "shoulds" for some people. Seeing a list of values that are supposedly common to others can make us feel like we should value them too – even if we don't. If you notice yourself having this reaction, I encourage you to gently remind your brain that it's okay; you're allowed to hold whatever values you have, and you are equally allowed not to value something.

Other lists of values are overwhelmingly long. They have the advantage of not limiting our possibilities but the disadvantage of leaving people unable to sift through what is important to them and what isn't. It can be difficult to notice which things are important to us and which are not when there are so many to choose from. Again, deductive approaches aren't right or wrong – just one way of identifying values that come with their advantages and disadvantages.

Inductive approaches involve observing ourselves and our lives to build a theory of our values. Instead of beginning with a list, we begin by noticing ourselves: What we like and dislike about ourselves, others, and the world around us, and how our bodies and emotions react to situations (both positively and negatively). What activities do we engage in to find meaning and joy, and which ones leave us bored and irritated? What do we love doing, and what do we hate? We can also draw on historical information from our past – what did we enjoy doing when we were younger? I've included below, in Figure 2.1, a list of the questions we often begin with when we're running workshops or working with coaching clients. I encourage you to pause and spend 15 minutes free writing your thoughts about any of these questions.

Inductive approaches have the advantage of not limiting us and being as open as possible when exploring our values. One disadvantage, however, is that they take time – they are a process and can take days, weeks, or months. They also require us to be good noticers of our internal states and external environment, which can take practice.

Given these advantages and disadvantages, the best way to build a model of what is important to us is often through a combination of deductive and inductive approaches. Deductive approaches can be a great place to get us started with some ideas about our core values. Inductive approaches can help us refine those ideas over time as we observe our lives in "real time" and see

Inductively identifying values

What makes you feel most engaged?

What does the perfect day look like?

When do you experience flow?

What would you get up at 3am for?

What makes you tired "in a good way"?

What gives you strong emotional reactions?

What is your fave way to spend money?

How did you play as a child?

Have you given up anything fun?

Figure 2.1 Questions to help inductively identify values

the match between our deductive inklings and our day-to-day experiences. Each can provide different information. But before we get to that, let's take a little detour to talk about emotions.

The Role of Emotions (and the Body) in Values Work

I noted earlier how our bodies and emotions react to situations (both positively and negatively). These reactions can be a source of information about our values. I encourage you to practice taking a little break to notice, throughout your day, what you are feeling emotionally and in your body as you work on identifying your core values.

Emotions are designed to provide information to us. They all serve a purpose. Emotions are also morally neutral. For example, feeling anger might be an indication that we do not like a situation or that our boundaries are being compromised. Boredom, impatience, and irritation (and accompanying bodily sensations) are three emotional signs that I am not doing values-consistent work. If I am on a committee and this is how meetings make me feel, it's a sign this is not the right committee for me. And yes, I have quit committees because this is how the meetings made me feel. As another example, frustration with students is often a message for me that my teaching style or assignments are not clicking with the class and that I need to adjust.

If you struggle to identify your emotions, do not fret. Many of us were not taught how to do it. Or we might be avoiding our emotions because we have beliefs that are making it harder for us to identify and feel them, such as, "I can't handle my emotions" or "I shouldn't be letting emotions get in the way of my work" or "I'll lose control if I pay attention to how I'm feeling". Emotions will come and go for all of us; this is a typical human experience. Sometimes, the best we can do is identify "this feels good" and "this feels bad", and that's good enough. To help you practice, I've included a feelings wheel below, in Figure 2.2.

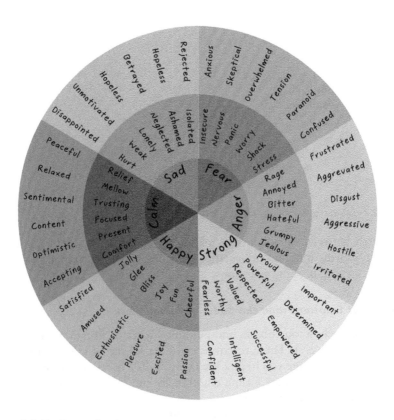

Figure 2.2 Feelings wheel

Like our emotions, our bodies also respond to situations – often so subtly that it's difficult to notice. Are there situations where your jaw feels tense? Are you clenching your teeth? When do you pull your shoulders up to your ears and keep them there? Are there situations where your body has a fear reaction – heart racing, breathing a bit faster, or more shallow than usual? There might also be positive bodily sensations that indicate you might be doing values-consistent activities: feeling calm and settled, loose feelings in your body, or comforting warmth in your chest.

For example, let me tell you about my "meeting ears". There is one committee that has long triggered my meeting ears: By the end of every meeting of this committee, my ears are bright red and feel like they are burning. This is often accompanied by fatigue – it's not uncommon for me to lie down after these committee meetings and need some quiet alone time. Suffice it to say, my body is very good at making me aware it does not like this committee. Listening to my body's messages, I've been able to adjust and introduce some habits that make it easier for me to attend this committee. For example, I join remotely from my home office as much as possible, I make myself tea, I wear comfy clothes, and I keep my camera off when its extra tough to be there.

Higher education encourages us to be a "brain on a stick" (i.e., ignores the fact that we are human beings with bodies and biological needs) (Faas, 2021), so it's not uncommon for those of us in academia to need a little bit more practice learning to pay attention to our bodies. If this is something new or challenging, be kind to yourself and keep practicing. Like most skills, the more we practice, the easier it gets.

Remember all those messages we discussed in the Introduction that higher education sends us? "Pay attention to your emotions and your body" is not one of them. Working in higher education, we are more often encouraged to avoid and suppress our emotions for the sake of productivity. Moreover, tone policing[1] dissent (i.e., telling others to "remain calm" to be heard) is frequent in higher education. It further encourages us to remain unemotional and detached from our feelings.

To help you practice identifying your bodily sensations, I've included a body scan script in Figure 2.3. If you prefer audio, there are many options on YouTube if you search "body scan".

Last, I want to introduce you to an idea that might seem a little bit woo (for those of you who are prone to being anti-woo, hang in there): Sometimes our bodies and our minds have access to information and have "opinions" that we can't necessarily put into words. My therapist and I use the term "body no" for this situation when it happens to me. These are situations in which I know I don't want to do something, but I do not have an intellectual or cognitive explanation for why. In the words of my therapist: "We don't have to be able to put something into words for it to be valid". My body is saying no, and that's sufficient.

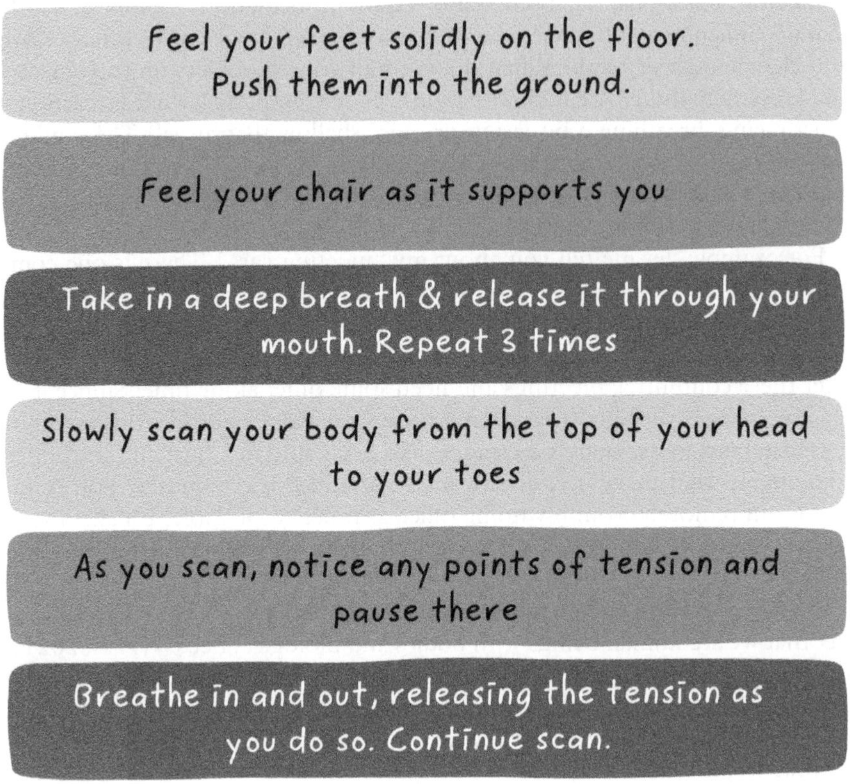

Feel your feet solidly on the floor.
Push them into the ground.

Feel your chair as it supports you

Take in a deep breath & release it through your mouth. Repeat 3 times

Slowly scan your body from the top of your head to your toes

As you scan, notice any points of tension and pause there

Breathe in and out, releasing the tension as you do so. Continue scan.

Figure 2.3 Body scan

A Combined Deductive-Inductive Approach to Identifying Values

After you've done the Valued Living Questionnaire and spent some time free writing responses to the inductive questions provided, I encourage you to take the time for this combined deductive-inductive approach to identifying values. This activity will refine the information you gained from the questionnaire and the free writing into a personalized list of values and definitions you will repeatedly return to for the remainder of the book (and hopefully beyond).

As we begin doing this vital work, I want to note that it might be challenging and bring up difficult memories, emotions, or experiences. By the time you get through this exercise you might notice you have values that aren't reflected in your life or your career – and that's hard. For example, aligning my career with my values has involved grief and mourning for things I thought would be part of my career that aren't or experiences that I thought I would love and didn't. In Dr. Jessica Campoli's dissertation work, which she completed in my lab, she found that before healthcare trainees began prioritizing self-care, they experienced "wake-up calls" where they realized their values and self-care were not aligned. This can be a painful awareness for some, bringing up big emotions that can be hard to experience.

I encourage you, going into this section, to plan how to be comfortable and make it as easy on yourself as possible. Light that expensive candle and find a comfortable and quiet location to do it. Snuggle with a pet. Use that gorgeous notebook you have. Take the day off and spend it on values work. Use your favorite pen. Take as many breaks as you need. Split this work across as many sittings as you need. Do the work with a trusted loved one. If you find this work is bringing up emotions that are too much to manage on your own, I encourage you to find a therapist or counselor to do it with.

Here we go!

First, review the list of values in Figure 2.4 (adapted from Goralewicz, n.d.). Don't do anything yet; just read through them. Some will stand out to you,

abundance	acceptance	advancement	adventure	affection
assertiveness	authenticity	balance	beauty	brilliance
calm	career	caring	challenge	comfort
commonality	conformity	cooperation	courage	creativity
curiosity	diversity	effectiveness	encourage	endurance
energy	enjoyment	entertain	entrepreneur	equality
excellence	facilitation	fairness	faith	fame
family	ferocious	finesse	fun	generosity
goodness	grace	gratitude	harmony	health
home	honesty	humanity	humor	humility
imagination	industry	independence	innovation	insight
integrity	intelligence	intimacy	intuition	inquisitive
invention	involvement	joy	justice	kindness
knowledge	leadership	learning	longevity	loyalty
love	mindfulness	order	open-minded	patience
peace	persistence	playfulness	pleasure	power
pride	professionalism	prosperity	quality	reciprocity
renewal	respect	responsibility	romance	safety
security	self-awareness	self-control	sensuality	sexuality
spaciousness	spirituality	skillfulness	stewardship	strength
success	supportiveness	sustainability	teamwork	trust
wealth	willingness	wisdom	youthful	zestful

Figure 2.4 (Nonexhaustive!) List of possible values

some you've probably never thought about, and some will make you think, "That's a value people have?!". Notice your responses (non-judgmentally). Remember, all your responses are fine and morally neutral.

Second, go through this list again slowly. Jot down the values that resonate with you on a separate paper. (Or you can highlight them directly in this book).[2] It's important to note that you don't have to know *why* they resonate with you. Remember: some knowledge is body knowledge. Intuition is a valid and helpful source of information.

As a caution, I want you to know that this exercise can make it easy to set your brain on autopilot. That's why I encourage you to go slowly and really consider each value and how you react to it cognitively, emotionally, and physiologically. When we're on autopilot, we can quickly begin highlighting values that we think we "should" have or sound nice, which won't be helpful for you when you apply this list later. Save yourself the extra work now and go slow and thoughtfully. This is also why I encourage you to remember that there are no right or wrong values and that only YOU can decide what you consider important. Take your time. Likewise, if there is a value or word that you don't see on this list that is important to you or resonates with you, feel free to add it.

In the third step, we will begin to sort and organize those values you highlighted or jotted down as potentially important to you. You might have chosen

Figure 2.5 Sort the values that resonate with you into groups that feel right

Photo by Brands&People, available on Unsplash at https://unsplash.com/photos/white-green-and-orange-box-RPPdQVp-nds

a lot of them – more than we could ever prioritize in one lifetime! That's okay. In this step, you might realize some of them aren't as important to you as you expected, and you might toss them out – that's perfectly okay too, and to be expected in this process.

On a separate piece of paper, begin "lumping together" (yes, that's my scientific label) value words that seem to fit together TO YOU. (Researcher nerd alert: This might be a familiar task if you have done any thematic analysis). Again, you don't need to understand why the values lump together. (There is no one coming to grade this assignment). You are sorting these into groups, encompassing the core or essential value that brings them together and makes them important to you. Again, don't be concerned about whether or not your lumpings would make sense to anyone else or if you can't explain why you think they fit together. Your lumps are yours, not anyone else's! You might end up with a pile of "miscellaneous" values that don't seem to go anywhere, and that's okay. This might also be something that you need to pause and come back to later. There is no rush, and revisiting your values exercises later is a great decision.

As an example, I've shared the "lumps" for three of my values in Table 2.1. When I created these lumps, I could not explain to you in words how they all fit together; a lot of this was just a feeling or intuition. They feel right to me this way.

Table 2.1 Jorden's Lumps and Associated Value Words

Lump #1	Lump #2	Lump #3
Brilliance	Comfort & Contentment	Family
Creativity	Energy	Ferocious
Imagination	Enjoyment	Generosity
Inquisitive	Health	Peace
Insightful	Love	Stewardship
Playfulness	Spaciousness	Sustainability
	Wealth	
	Longevity	

Once you have sorted your value words, the fourth step is to create a label for that "lump" of values. The label might be one of the words that stands out as a great label for the whole group, a term they all seem to relate to, or a nonsensical label that only makes sense to you. Again, the label only needs to make sense to you, no one else. When I do this exercise, I use gerunds to help capture a sense of movement or action for my labels. This is a good reminder of matching actions (i.e., behaviors) to my values – it helps me generate activities and behaviors derived from my values. Do whatever works for you. Remember: You're the boss, applesauce.

As an example, here are those lumps of words I had with the labels I generated for them, in Table 2.2:

Table 2.2 Jorden's Labels for Value Lumps

Creating Beauty	Richness of Life	Connection (Interspecies, Human, & Nature)
Brilliance	Comfort & Contentment	Family
Creativity	Energy	Ferocious
Imagination	Enjoyment	Generosity
Inquisitive	Health	Peace
Insightful	Love	Stewardship
Playfulness	Spaciousness	Sustainability
	Wealth	
	Longevity	

The fifth and final step is to define what this value means for you in the context of YOUR life. How would you define it? I know I am hammering home this point a lot, but there are no right or wrong, correct or incorrect definitions for your values. All of this is highly personal and morally neutral. Essentially, I am asking you to answer the question: What does this value mean to you and look like in your life?

It's essential to anchor your definition in your understanding of your life because it will help you derive self-care activities (and work choices) from that definition later. At the same time, we're not aiming for perfection. You might come back and revise this definition later, and that's fine too.

Once again, here are mine in Table 2.3 as an example:

Table 2.3 Jorden's Definition of Core Values

Core Value	Jorden's Definition
Creating Beauty	Giving beautiful things back to the world and enjoying the beauty around me. Fueling my curious nature with learning and new activities, and fostering a sense of play. Beauty includes order and cleanliness in my physical space
Richness of Life	Creating a life that reflects who I am and what I want. Including a balance of comfort and joy, spaciousne to explore who I am, and creating generational wealth to care for my child
Connection (Interspecies, Human, & Nature)	Being connected with people, nature, and Creator. Using my privilege to give back and focus on sustainability in connections, nature, and lifestyle. Practicing good relations.

Changing Seasons, Changing Value Priorities

I wrote part of this chapter at a writing retreat, where I overlooked a big open field and a pine tree that I've grown to love and connect with at the retreat location – a place I've been to many times. It was overcast on the first writing day, and the field was gloomy. On the second day, the field was full of sunshine, except under that beautiful pine tree where it was shaded. The last day, the field was foggy and encased in hoarfrost. When I returned in the early Spring for another writing retreat, all the snow was gone. I watched a magpie come and go from the pine tree, and my colleague and I enjoyed walking along the gravel paths for a break. I watched as some-one harvested rhubarb from a patch in the middle of that field – a patch I didn't even notice in the Winter. The following Fall, when I was revising this chapter, it was exceptionally warm and there was no snow at all – just brown grass.

There is much to abstract about values from my experiences with "my" field. First, while the weather and the field's appearance can change from sea-son to season or even daily, the field is still there. Like the field, our core values are always there. Also, like the field, our days and months shift with the seasons of our lives. Likewise, different values will take priority in different seasons of our lives.

For example, being a present parent who promotes secure attachment with my child is a core value for me. Was this always my intention? Absolutely. But before I had a child to parent, I didn't live this value in my day-to-day life.[3]

Just as the seasons of our lives change, our careers also change. Kerry Ann Roquemore, founder of the National Center for Faculty Development & Di-versity, labelled this concept as our careers being "books with many chapters". For example, in the first "chapter" of my tenure track career, I focused on publishing (or perishing), desperate for the security of a tenured position. I published anything and everything, and speed was critical! My second career chapter (post-tenure) focused on teaching and mentoring – I developed and taught various new courses and even curated/wrote two open educational resources (textbooks for Introductory Psychology and Abnormal Psychology) that I'm proud of. The third chapter of my career (which has just begun) is (so far) focused on research, community, and entrepreneurship.

Each career chapter has required me to emphasize specific values. Does it mean I've dropped or quit my other values? Not necessarily. But I am not as focused on them. I still think it's important to be a competent and committed instructor, but I do not center my career around this activity in this chapter.

We can't always give equal priority to each of our values in every season of our lives. We don't have the capacity. In my workshops and one-on-one work with graduate students, I often hear them describe feeling that their values conflict because of the pressure required to obtain a graduate degree. They desire and are striving toward that accomplishment, which involves a lot of sacrifice. For example, while graduate students might value strong connections with friends and family, they might also be in demanding pro-grams of study that leave them little time or energy to foster those connec-tions. In these situations, we sometimes need to choose which priority will receive the bulk of our energy and accept "good enough" for our other values – remembering, of course, that how we build these priorities and allocate our energy is up to us. Again, there are no right or wrong ways to prioritize.

Many people experienced these seasons of values or need to prioritize values differently during the early stages of the COVID-19 pandemic, especially during the months when many of us were required to stay home as a public safety measure. Further, many people noticed their values more prominently in their lives during this time – for some, being kept at home blocked access to how they usually express their values (for example, people whose valued living is obtained via travel). For others, and I fall into this category, the time at home allowed us to clarify our values, perhaps because we were without our usual distractions and because of the existential threat posed by pandemics. I have emerged these years later with a much clearer sense of my values and a stronger push to align my life with them.

Conclusion (TL;DR, But I Hope You Read)

In this chapter, we defined values and linked our definition to the concepts of valued living (i.e., living a life consistent with our values) and committed action (i.e., our values reflected in our actions and behaviors). You learned deductive, inductive, and combined methods for uncovering your core values and defining what they mean to you. That's a lot of internal work; not everyone takes the time to do it, so please pat yourself on the back. Do whatever soothing you need to do. Feel accomplished and proud! We also discussed how our priorities must change in various seasons of our lives. Having set the stage, let's learn about what self-care is, what it's not, and how to use your core values (capitalizing on self-determination theory) to derive self-care choices from those values.

Notes

1 Tone policing is "the rejection of an argument on the grounds of the tone in which it is delivered rather than on the grounds of its content" (Collins, n.d.). Dominant groups tone policing minority groups is a tactic of oppression.
2 Allowing myself to see my books as tools and permitting myself to mark them up was an important career turning point for me! Also, it's liberating. But don't do it to library books or books you borrowed!
3 Instead, I had only my cat lady values to live by – now I have both.

References

Collins. (n.d.). Tone policing. In *Collins.com* dictionary. Retrieved December 30, 2023, from https://www.collinsdictionary.com/dictionary/english/tone-policing

Faas, C. (2021). *Unstuck: Three-step system to help high achievers move from stress to flow.* Independently published.

Goralewicz, O. (n.d.). A full list of values for Acceptance and Commitment Therapy (ACT). *Loving health.* https://loving.health/en/act-list-of-values/

Wilson, K. G., & DuFrene, T. (2009). *Mindfulness for two: An acceptance and commitment therapy approach to mindfulness in psychotherapy.* New Harbinger.

Chapter 3

Using Values to Guide Your Self-Care

What Self-Care Is and What Self-Care Is Not

Self-care is a hot topic these days. It's especially hot on social media. I recently read an article speculating that "self-care" was the most searched term on Google in all of 2020! Academia is not immune to these influences, and it warms my heart to see more discussions of how we can thrive and be well in our industry. My quick search of "self-care higher education" garnered 1.49 *billion* results.

Self-care is a term that can include a vast range of behaviors, choices, lifestyles, and even products (Lakshmin, 2023). Scholars and practitioners use many definitions of self-care, and later in this chapter, I'll share with you the one we've developed in my lab. For now, needs a space you can think of self-care as anything you choose to do to maintain your health and well-being.

To understand self-care, it is helpful to know its origins and uses. Self-care is a phrase that has some of its roots in Western medicine, from the 1950s. It was used to refer to the behaviors and strategies physicians and other health care providers wanted their patients to use to best look after themselves, often post-diagnosis or surgical intervention. For example, patients who have experienced a heart attack would be advised to engage in self-care by changing their diet, decreasing their stress, and perhaps taking certain medications. Patients with diabetes would be advised to pay attention to what they eat, take their insulin, and exercise regularly. In pharmacy, self-care can refer to the medicines that patients and customers receive and pharmacists' role in ensuring patients know how to use them correctly (Bell, Dziekan, Pollack, & Mahachai, 2016).

Eventually, within medicine and other healthcare professions, self-care came to refer to the behaviors and strategies professionals use to care for themselves. That is, self-care transitioned from a term physicians and other health professionals used to refer to what they expected patients to do into one that also referred to how they need to look after themselves as helping professionals. This is often linked to health and helping professionals' responsibility to provide the safest and best care for their clients or patients. The ethics codes of many health care professionals, like the North American codes for psychologists,

DOI: 10.4324/9781003379805-4

were adapted to explicitly include the expectation that they engage in self-care. Healthcare providers who work while impaired by stress, burnout, or other concerns associated with these professions can seriously harm clients and patients via medical mistakes or unethical decision-making – hence the ethical obligation to ensure that they look after their well-being to provide competent care.

It is critical to acknowledge (and express gratitude for) the role that BIPOC activists have had in shaping our concepts of self-care. Self-care and community care can be synonymous in this context. For example, the community health care and education opportunities that the Black Panthers set up in the 1960s are examples of **radical self-care**. According to the School of Art Institute of Chicago, radical self-care is "the prioritization of placing your needs before someone else's. Radical self-care is carving out a space for yourself by defining your own self-care" (School of the Art Institute of Chicago, n.d.). By taking control of their community and individual health and wellness, activists engaged in (and are still engaging in) radical self-care as an act of resistance (School of the Art Institute of Chicago, n.d.). In higher education, where institutions and systems do not often value self-care, prioritizing it can also be an act of resistance. We should place self-care at the heart of our work, which best positions us to help others.

The famous Audre Lorde quote, "Caring for myself is not self-indulgence, it is self-preservation, and that is an act of political warfare", provides an example of how self-care was used to protest and push back against oppression for Black communities (Lorde, 2017).

Unfortunately, self-care is also a term that has been tragically commodified by capitalism. For example, any online search for self-care advice will inevitably lead to an array of products and services whose advertising tells you they are the key to your self-care. **The global wellness industrial complex is worth over $5.6 trillion** (Global Wellness Institute, 2023). Pooja Lakshmin terms these types commodified of self-care "faux self-care" (2023). Faux self-care refers to "products and solutions marketed to us as remedies" (p. xiv) that are "largely full of empty calories and devoid of substance. [They] keep us looking outward – comparing ourselves to others or striving for a certain type of perfection – which means [they are] incapable of truly nourishing us in the long run" (p. xiv). For example, in our research on how social media influencers portray self-care, we found that much of the shared content supported a maladaptive diet culture[1] (Knowles & Cummings, 2023).

When our motivation for how we treat ourselves and our bodies stems from unrealistic beauty standards placed upon us by others or from comparing our bodies to others, the resulting choices are arguably not self-care but rather **faux** self-care. We captured just how commodified self-care can be (as portrayed by YouTube influencers) (Knowles & Cummings, 2023). Those influencers centered their self-care around expensive experiences and products (e.g., spa days, skincare routines, particular clothing) and framed them as necessary for everyone's lives. At the same time, these self-care practices were unattainable by the average person who would neither have time for the elaborate routines nor the necessary disposable income for the products (and no sponsors or advertisers to buy them) (Knowles & Cummings, 2023). A quick search on social media or any online shopping site will reveal several multi-billion dollar industries that center at least some of their products and services around (allegedly) self-care: vacations, candles, clothes, adventure sports, cars, bath bombs, cell phones… you name it, there is probably a "self-care" (scare quotes on purpose) version of that product out there.

This is not how self-care should be. The self-care discussed in this book is born from an anti-capitalist, anti-oppressive approach to self-care. It is aligned with the radical self-care definition discussed above. Moreover, I'm sorry to say while bath bombs can be relaxing to watch and smell nice, no bath bomb can fully substitute for quality self-care.

Our Definition of Self-Care

There are many ways that people define self-care, some more complicated than others. I like simplicity. The definition we've developed in our lab is this: **Self-care is anything you do to replenish your personal and/or professional selves** (recognizing that these are not truly separate selves).

The key word in this definition is *replenish*. When it comes to our choices, we can do things that use energy or replenish our energy – the ones that replenish are what we will label self-care.

This definition is purposefully broad, and that's for two reasons. First, we want to make clear that there are no specific behaviors or tasks that "count" as self-care and others that don't. Almost anything can be self-care. No research supports one specific task over another for self-care (Campoli & Cummings, 2023; Colman et al., 2016). By keeping the definition broad, we emphasize that the sky is the limit when it comes to self-care choices. What works as self-care for one person won't necessarily work for someone else, and vice versa.

The other advantage of this broad definition is that you are probably already doing a lot of self-care behaviors that you might not have labeled as such. With our definition focused on *replenishment*, self-care can include activities like vacations, walking in nature, and, yes, taking a bubble bath, with or without a bath bomb. But it can also include brushing our teeth, paying our bills, and taking our medication. Sometimes self-care doesn't even feel good – but ultimately, it's still replenishing because it takes care of us … like going for a colonoscopy if you are as old as I am.

This definition is anti-capitalist because it does not require purchasing anything to fulfill your self-care needs. We can engage in self-care in many ways that do not cost money. Some quick examples from my life: reading books from the library, getting the amount of sleep my body needs, and going for a walk in the autumn leaves.

What's Wrong with Traditional Approaches to Self-Care

The way that most recommendations for those of us in higher education approach self-care is completely wrong. That's not a statement I make lightly as a psychology researcher since we're taught to tread lightly with our claims, but after more than a decade of working in the self-care space, I feel confident saying it.

First, self-care recommendations are way too prescriptive. A lot of self-care advice, even that which is peer-reviewed, consists of "grocery lists" of activities that you can and supposedly should engage in for self-care, without even considering what might be appealing to you or fit in your actual life. They often use narrow definitions of self-care (e.g., "walking 10,000 steps per day") or set broad domains (e.g., "physical self-care"). None of this approach is individualized or tailored to the specific needs, preferences, and lifestyles of individuals, who are not all the same.

Second, none of us are trained in self-care. Very few to no aspects of education at any level focus on self-care. Even in the health and helping professions, where self-care is an ethical requirement, few training programs provide self-care-related education. Not only are we not trained in self-care, but it is also poorly modeled – often by people telling us we need to engage in it. While many of us in higher education received training or professional degrees to do our jobs, none of that training likely involved self-care practices. And for the programs that discuss self-care (like my discipline, clinical psychology – although you can still do an entire degree without hearing about self-care at some institutions), the messages are often so mixed that no trainee even believes what they are being told – it has zero credibility. The same thing can happen now with our employers – they can tell us to engage in self-care but then overload us with so much work or take away all of our support to the point where their messages about self-care are confusing and possibly meaningless. We expect them to know better, but they often don't.

Third, traditional approaches to self-care are often reactive, blaming, or fear-based. For example, self-care is recommended when someone is burnt out, impaired, or not performing their job at the expected level of competency. The underlying message of that approach is that self-care is punishment for incompetence and that only struggling people need to engage in it. Instead, self-care should be something we are all encouraged to participate in regardless of our stress levels. It should proactively be used to promote a wonderful life worth living. Moreover, self-care as the solution for individual burnout downloads responsibility for worker wellness to that individual, when we all know that our work context plays a huge role in our well-being. As Pooja Lakshim notes in *Real Self-Care,* "when you don't find time for these 'solutions,' it's your fault for not keeping up with one more task on your to-do list" (p. xiii). Self-care can feel like one more burden we're behind on and feel guilty for not doing, which is not helpful. Lakshim refers to this as the "tyranny of self-care" (2023, p. 5).

Self-care messaging often revolves around what we might risk or lose if we do not engage in it (i.e., fear-based) rather than what we might gain from it. For example, in my field (clinical psychology), self-care is an ethical imperative. So, we receive the message that if we don't engage in self-care bad things will happen (we will provide unethical care, we will be sued and lose our license and thus our livelihood) rather than emphasizing what we gain from being in a place of balanced wellness: Full engagement in our life, improved well-being, and joy. Spoiler alert! No one is motivated by fear in the long term. Choosing to pursue self-care activities from this mindset makes them feel like a chore we are behind on and tends to lead to us giving up on those activities altogether. We are only motivated by fear for so long. As we'll discuss more in later chapters focusing on what we will gain is the best way to approach our self-care.

Last, much of the messaging we receive about traditional approaches to self-care is not evidence-based. While opinion and case examples are great, at the end of the day we want our self-care recommendations to have some evidence behind them. Moreover, self-care recommendations should be held to the same standard as other health interventions. Just like we would not want our therapist to be using interventions no one had determined would be helpful or our doctor prescribing medications not demonstrated to work for our illness, we do not want to receive recommended self-care strategies willy-nilly with no evidence they might help.

Self-Care vs. Soothing

Unfortunately, many messages and models about self-care conflate two distinct concepts: Self-care and soothing. We've already defined self-care as anything you can do to replenish your personal and/or professional selves. Soothing behaviors, in contrast, are those you choose to do to regulate (often decrease) your physiological arousal. For example, punching a pillow when you feel angry, using that bath bomb to calm down after an upsetting day of work, going for a walk, or calling a friend to vent are all soothing.

Both soothing and self-care are fantastic. Soothing can help us out when we've had a tough day, relax our nervous system, and just feel good. There is a place for soothing in our self-care, but soothing alone is insufficient. While soothing can help us feel good in the moment, self-care often requires more than soothing to be effective. For example, if we're working so many hours at our job that we have no time left to get enough sleep or go to the doctor or see our family (or whatever values-consistent self-care choice works for you), no amount of soothing (e.g., bubble baths, binge-watching television) will make that situation change. If we're being bullied by a colleague and no one will intervene to help, and we're thinking of quitting... a glass of wine after work will not resolve that situation.

This brings us back to our discussion of the commodification of self-care: What is often commodified are products that help with soothing. The self-care industrial complex wants to sell us all kinds of products for pleasant experiences: Shampoos, facemasks, make-up, clothes, diet and exercise plans, pills, sauna blankets, cruises... I could go on and on and on. Many of these will be soothing – but that doesn't necessarily make them *replenishing*, especially in the long term. Values and self-care are not commodities. We need to be critical thinkers when it comes to our self-care choices.[2]

Deriving Self-Care From Your Core Values

At this point, we've discussed what's hard about working in higher education, why values can be an important compass, and how to identify our core values. We've outlined a definition of self-care and distinguished between soothing and self-care. It's time to use those values to inform our self-care choices.

Creating Values-Informed Self-Care Plans

It's time to use the core values you identified in Chapter 2, including the definitions you gave them, to develop self-care plans. In Chapter 4, we'll do the same thing to create a framework to refine our approach to work.

The key to values-informed self-care plans is simple: Use your self-care time to engage in behaviors that are consistent with, and move you toward, your values.[3] Remember, we are pulling from self-determination theory and using our values to stack the self-care deck in our favor. When you engage in values-consistent self-care activities, you will find them easier to make time for, feel more motivated to engage in them and experience more benefits from them.

Anyone who has attended one of my self-care talks or workshops knows that I love to use running to illustrate the power of values-aligned self-care choices. In my experience, running produces strong reactions in most people. For some, this strong reaction is joy. Others feel strongly that running is not something they enjoy, nor are they interested in beginning a running practice. Still others feel strongly ambivalent about running.

I live in Saskatoon, Saskatchewan. Saskatoon is often referred to as one of the sunniest cities in Canada. In the summer we have long beautiful days of sun, with the sun rising very early and setting very late. It is a beautiful city for someone to begin and maintain a running practice. And based on my observations when I am out and about, we have a lot of runners in Saskatoon.

However, in the Winter, Saskatoon has a lot of dark and often deep cold. At its latest, the sun rises after many of us have gone to work for the day and sets before we have left. At its absolute coldest, with windchill, our temperatures are comparable to Mars.

Engaging in a running practice in Saskatoon in the Winter is still possible, but it requires the right equipment. You need layers that can keep you warm while sweating. Shoes with spikes that will grip the ice. That is, once the Winter hits, there are barriers to continuing a running practice. But some people will still do it. I would argue that those are the people for whom running is a values-aligned self-care activity. Investing in the appropriate running gear and getting yourself out in the dark and the cold requires a lot of motivation – and that motivation will come much easier to those for whom running is a self-determined behavior with a clear why (i.e., value) behind it.

Self-care activities that give you the same motivation to accomplish them as a Winter outdoor runner in Saskatoon, Saskatchewan, are the self-care activities we seek. What values-aligned self-care choices would motivate you as much as the runner out at 6 am in –25 degrees Celsius running on ice? That's what we are aiming for![4]

It is important to note that figuring out your self-care likes and dislikes is a process. It's not something that happens overnight. We need to try things, see how they work for us, notice our reactions to them, and either toss out that idea out or continue. This is a great process to bring your creativity to (and most of us working in higher education have great creative skills, whether you label them as such or not). Learning what self-care activities you dislike is as essential as learning which ones you like. (Dislikes for me: yoga, group-based exercise, meditation, for example). Learning how to tweak, alter, and adapt the activities to work for you (more on that later) is just as important as learning which ones you like.

I will tell you the three basic steps to this process, and then I will illustrate it with some examples from my experiences. Figure 3.1 outlines all of the steps.

Step 1 is deciding on some behaviors to try. As a way to get started, I invite you to set a timer for 10-15 minutes and brainstorm some ways you can use self-care to move toward your values using Table 3.1. It will be helpful here for you to refer back to your specific definitions of self-care to tailor your ideas as much as possible. The more we can capitalize on self-determination theory, the more likely we are stacking the deck in our favor for actually finding time to do self-care.

Table 3.1 Values and Potential Consistent Self-Care Behaviors

Core Value	Potential Self-Care Behaviors

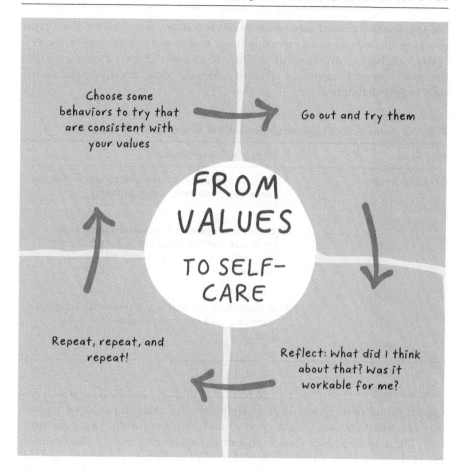

Figure 3.1 Steps to identifying values-based self-care activities

Step 2 is going out and trying them! After all, we won't know if we like something if we don't try it.

Step 3 requires reflecting on our choices over time to decide if they are workable for us or options that aren't best for us. This process requires trial and error and practice over time.

Self-care is more than just a set of behaviors or activities; it is also the journey of self-discovery to learn about ourselves and how to best care for our unique selves. Embarking on this journey is building a new relationship with yourself. That relationship and your identity as someone who cares for yourself (Campoli & Cummings, 2024) is just as important as the behaviors you try along the way.

As an example of deriving some self-care activities from values, Table 3.2 shows my self-care ideas for my value that I've labeled "Creating Beauty".

You can see that my self-care activities and behaviors move beyond short-term soothing and include things you might not traditionally think of as "self-care". If you look back to my definitions of my values from Chapter 2, you'll see that the behaviors and activities I've chosen include some directly linked to my own unique definitions.

Table 3.2 Jorden's Self-Care Activities for the Value "Creating Beauty"

Core Value	Potential Self-Care Behaviors
Creating Beauty	Artistic activities that allow me to work with my hands (e.g., coloring, Lego, pottery)
	Routines and systems that allow me to keep my house tidy with minimal effort from me. This includes spending money on a house cleaner
	Not overfilling my non-work time with scheduled activities, so I can create space for "dream time"

As you might expect for a value related to creating and beauty (which had related values of imagination and playfulness, for example), a lot of my self-care ideas include artistic and creative endeavors: coloring, Lego, and pottery. But it also includes choices that might not seem obvious, like ensuring my space is clean and tidy. To me, this feels beautiful (as well as calm and soothing). Having a tidy space physically, as well as in my calendar via white space and not being overscheduled, also serves the purpose of freeing my mind to be creative rather than distracted by – and thus focused on – mess and overwhelm. Doing so also leaves time in my schedule to pursue creativity, personally and professionally. For example, as someone who craves order and tidiness, it would be difficult for me to make time for art on a random Tuesday afternoon if my house was dirty – I would use that time to clean. Thus, keeping my house tidy provides me with the time to engage in creative activities.

"Why not just accept that the house is dirty and do art anyway" you might be wondering. This is common and completely valid advice. However, I've learned through my self-care journey, self-discovery, and changing relationship with myself that this is not feasible advice **for me**. That doesn't mean it's not feasible for you. Remember, you're the boss of what works for you. And whatever works (or does not work) for you is completely okay.

Here is another example from my value of Connection, in Table 3.3.

Table 3.3 Jorden's Self-Care Activities for the Value "Connection"

Core Value	Potential Self-Care Behaviors
Connection (Interspecies, Human, Nature)	Regularly connecting with close friends
	Making time for conversation and play with my child
	Gardening and reading about gardening and other sustainability practices
	Brushing my cats while I drink my morning tea
	Letting my cats sleep on me while I read or work

As you will see in my example, there are several self-care activities that move me toward my value of Connection, consistent with my unique definition that includes interspecies connection, connecting with other humans, and connecting with nature. You might also value connection but have a completely different personal definition of what that means to you – which, again, is absolutely amazing and perfectly okay. That means that you would likely have different self-care behaviors in mind to match your definition.

Between the number of values any person might have and the unique ways they can define that value for themselves, there is probably an infinite number of self-care possibilities. I see that as fantastic because it means there are self-care behaviors that each of us can get excited about as individuals (like those Winter runners in their layers, running in the dark).

Assessing the Function of a Behavior to Know If It's Self-Care

When doing workshops, it's common for attendees to ask questions about specific self-care choices and whether they are "right" or "wrong". As an example, I distinctly remember an excellent question from a faculty member during a webinar that demonstrates the critical need to understand how the function of a behavior determines if it is self-care.

This faculty member described to me how one of her favorite ways to engage in self-care was to take her laptop to a coffee shop near her office, meet up with her friend from work, and for them to write together. (I think I remember this question so clearly because this is also one of my favorite professional self-care activities!). The faculty member asked me: Is this self-care, or can it not be self-care because it involves work? Said differently: can work be self-care?

To answer this question, I responded with a question of my own: When engaging in this choice, did she feel replenished or drained? The faculty member quickly stated that she found this activity restorative – not only was she being productive, but she also got to do so with her friend. She loved the environment of the coffee shop. We easily concluded that working in this context was a self-care choice for this particular person.

This example is a good reminder that **whether or not something replenishes us is key to understanding if it is self-care**. It also illustrates an important distinction about self-care, why there is no sense in prescribing particular activities, and the role of context in understanding our behavioral choices: The same behavior could be self-care for one person and poor coping for another. For example, while my workshop attendee loves working in a coffee shop with her friend and finds it replenishing, someone else in the same situation might choose to work in a coffee shop because they feel anxious and behind and are desperately motivated by fear of failure, and going to the office causes too much stress. Some people live and breathe by their yoga practice, and yoga is an activity that makes me feel awkward and uncomfortably self-conscious and not at all replenished. I know many people who find coffee a soothing part of their day. If I'm drinking more than one coffee per day, it's a sign I'm anxious about something. I could go on and on – any choice can be self-care for one person, and the opposite of self-care, or completely neutral for another – and that is perfectly, perfectly fine.

Not only can the same behavior be self-care for one person and not for another, but the same behavior could be self-care for ourselves at one point and not self-care at another time or in another context. (This is particularly salient to me at this exact moment because I just turned on the news for "background noise" while I wrote this section, but eventually admitted I was just avoiding writing). Sometimes such background noise is really helpful for me, and other times it's not.[5]

To understand these differences, **we need to pay attention to the function of the behavior**. To do this, we need to notice what we think and how we feel by using the emotion and body skills that we talked about in Chapter 2. All of this reflection is part of our self-care journey and related to the steps I previously described of trying behaviors, evaluating our reactions, and either tweaking them or returning to the drawing board.

As an example, let's take a behavior that a lot of us can relate to: Binge-watching our preferred streaming service (or doom-scrolling on our phones). Sometimes this might be a self-care choice. Sometimes this might just be avoidance. How do we tell the difference? **It all depends on why and in what context we choose to do it.** If we're binge-watching our favorite show to be entertained (see, for example, me when a new season of Bridgerton is released) or scrolling our phone and laughing at hilarious TikTok videos to chill after a long day, our behavior is serving a much different function than if we are binge watching something to avoid thinking about a problem that makes us feel like crap or because we just want to numb out for a few hours. The critical distinction is the *purpose* (i.e., the function) of the behavior we choose to do. If behavior is consistent with our values, moving us toward them and replenishing us, then it's self-care. If it's inconsistent with our values, moving us away from them and neither soothing nor replenishing, then it might not be a helpful choice in that moment.

Lakshmin (2023) offers characteristics that identify potential faux self-care and can also help you delineate if a behavioral choice is helpfully serving you. She argues that faux self-care is usually motivated by one of three reasons: escape, achievement, or optimization. My example of doom scrolling social media to avoid thinking about our tough day at work is escape. As Lakshmin notes, "[u]sing self-care to escape our regular lives – while temporarily enjoyable – seldom results in lasting change" (p. 24). Faux self-care motivated by achievement is characterized by activities designed for success, involving comparing ourselves to others and stemming from a sense of worthlessness. For example, if you find yourself more invested in getting the "right" social media picture of an activity rather than whether it replenishes you, this might be an achievement goal pretending to be self-care. Last, optimization-focused faux self-care focuses on helping us live our lives faster, more efficiently, and *better*. While some optimization can improve self-care (As we'll discuss more in Chapter 4), understanding the **why** behind our strive to optimize is critical: "When you use efficiency as a coping mechanism to deal with the chaos of modern life, it's very easy to forget the real point of efficiency: to free up time and space for yourself. *Doing more does not always lead to feeling better*" (Lakshmin, 2023, p. 35). If you find yourself optimizing but still ruminating about how to do things even more efficiently instead of using your found time for self-care and enjoying life, you might be engaged in faux self-care. I've summarized the differences between self-care and avoidance in Figure 3.2.

Self-Care	Avoidance
Replenishing	Draining
Workable for us	Not workable for us
Entertaining	"Checking out"
Engaging	Escaping
Loving and accepting of who we are	Aimed at improving without acceptance

Figure 3.2 Is it self-care or avoidance?

This leads to our next important point to understand – there are no "right" (or wrong) self-care choices – only ones that work for you and ones that don't.

There Are No "Right" Choices, Just Workability

That sentence is so important that it bears repeating: There are no "right" self-care choices (that we "should" be doing), only ones that work for you and ones that don't. And whatever works for you is great – remember, our choices are morally neutral. There are no self-care police "out there" judging you for what you do

Figure 3.3 What matters the most is pursuing what's workable for you

Photo by Mansvita S., available on Unsplash at https://unsplash.com/photos/spiral-freestanding-calendar-on-white-surface-9q5vptiE2TY

to replenish yourself. The only important thing is whether your self-care choices work for you. And if they don't work for you? Then they're not that helpful. Said differently: Don't waste your time trying to engage in any self-care behavior because you "should", because you "have to", or because you believe other people think you should. **If a choice is unenjoyable, dreadful, or not even remotely aligned with your values, then just let it go** (and letting it go is a wonderful act of self-care!). As I told one of our early workshop audience members: You *can* bake cookies for your friends instead of exercise. It's all up to you.

Who gets to decide what's workable for you? You do! (And no one else). Again: You're the boss, applesauce! And what's workable for you doesn't have to be workable – or even make sense – to anyone else.

I encourage you to remind yourself regularly that there are no self-care police and get creative with determining what's workable for you. It can be liberating to realize you **don't have to do what you don't want to do.** You don't have to jog, put your laundry away, do yoga, eat kale, or have a bubble bath. You get to do whatever replenishes YOU.

Caveat: Self-Care Doesn't Always Feel Good

I will start this section with a small disclaimer: The following information might be a bit of a bummer, and for that I apologize. But it's also realistic.

Sometimes self-care doesn't feel good in the moment. Sometimes it feels good in the long term, but sometimes not. Sometimes doing what's value-aligned and what cares for ourselves is hard and unpleasant. That's okay – we can handle hard and unpleasant. For example, many of us engage in necessary self-care activities that don't feel particularly exciting or joyful, even if they are replenishing. Few of us get jazzed about brushing our teeth, paying our bills, and going for medical tests when we are worried something is wrong – those are all examples of self-care that we might not feel thrilled to do. Last year I had a breast biopsy, and that was no fun (I'm fine), but I do feel proud I looked after myself by doing it. (I'm also proud of myself for saying "Yes, please!" when they offered more numbing: 10/10, highly recommend). I also shared the example earlier in the book of engaging in activities my child loves that I don't find inherently captivating – I do them because I value being a present parent.[6]

If we think of self-care as only that which feels good in the moment, we're mistakenly focusing only on soothing. Self-care, as we've been discussing, encompasses much more. As previously mentioned, what capitalism has commodified is usually soothing – things that feel good in the moment. And then, when that moment fades, need to be replaced with more purchases to get another fleeting moment of feeling good...and repeat... this is how self-care contributes to that trillion-dollar industry: by keeping us continually chasing soothing. If this industry worked, we'd spend a chunk of money, our problem would be solved, and we'd never spend on self-care again! (And no one would profit from our problems). (Same as the diet industry).

Sometimes long-term self-care can also require shorter-term ~~sacrifice~~ choice[7]. For example, I am a person who needs about 9–10 hours of sleep per night to be my best. I have *always* been a person who needs a lot of sleep; this is unlikely to change. This is an excellent example of where people can be different. While I know people who feel completely rested after 7 or 8 hours of sleep, and I am very jealous of them, that amount leaves me feeling groggy and sleep-deprived. Too many nights of not enough sleep is not a good scene for me. I end up overly emotional, easily overstimulated, unable to focus, and I'm likely to get a migraine. It can be tricky to get all of the sleep I need, especially as a parent. Because I have decided getting enough sleep is core to my self-care, I have to make choices to make that happen. For example, I carve out time during the day for some of my self-care choices to make sure they happen. I go to bed early, which means I'm selective about what invitations I accept that happen at night. When I travel, I now avoid very early morning flights that will mess with my sleep, which sometimes means taking an extra day of travel to get somewhere. I often tell others my entire life is centered around getting enough sleep. I'm not joking. I will give up many things before I give up sleep.

You can see from my examples so far in this chapter that effective self-care practices involve knowing ourselves well. To develop workable self-care plans, we need to understand our values, preferences, and needs. As Lakshim (2023) notes: "[t]o practice real self-are, you must be willing to make yourself vulnerable – whether that means having uncomfortable conversations to set boundaries or making the clear and deliberate choice to prioritize one aspect of your life over another" (p. 76). This doesn't happen all at once. It's a journey that involves trial and error.

The Trial and Error of Developing Workable, Values-Informed Self-Care Habits

For part of her dissertation research in my lab, Dr. Jessica Campoli interviewed trainees enrolled in professional helping or healthcare programs (like medicine, nursing, psychology, education, or law) about how they developed successful self-care practices. Dr. Campoli found that values were embedded throughout this process. For example, her participants described being motivated to develop self-care practices after noticing a disconnect between their lifestyle and their core personal values. They then embarked on a journey of exploring self-care behaviors that might be consistent with those values over time.

Dr. Campoli also found two critical sub-processes for people as they developed and refined their self-care practices: (1) trial and error and (2) persistence in difficult times.

What Dr. Campoli found reinforces the ideas I've shared in this chapter about how discovering what self-care practices work best for us involves trying things, evaluating them, and then tweaking, discontinuing, or continuing them. This process has no specific timeline, and the journey is slightly different for everyone. But we cannot develop a workable self-care plan without actually trying stuff (i.e., committed action). Sometimes that stuff will turn out to be things we love, and sometimes maybe we hate. We won't know without experiencing them. "The most important thing for you to do is to take action. It doesn't have to be perfect. You don't have to know all of the steps you will take along the way. All you have to do is be willing to start. Commit to doing the work. The next steps will appear at the right time" (Kinsey, 2022, p. 15).

Participants in Dr. Campoli's study engaged in this process of trial and error, and it benefitted them by giving them self-care practice. The more they practiced, the easier self-care became. The more they practiced, the more they could refine their self-care practices to work for them. **There is no such thing as self-care failure, only self-care feedback.**

Dr. Campoli also found that participants who could engage in this practice and then **persist with self-care when it was difficult** benefitted greatly from that challenge. It can be easier to develop self-care ideas but not follow through with them – even harder to refine our self-care into workable, values-informed practices and then evaluate them. But the more refined we can be with our self-care plans, the more likely we are to follow through with them (hence, we want to use self-determination theory and values to stack the deck in our favor). The more likely we are to follow through with them, at least for the participants in Dr. Campoli's study, the more we begin to view ourselves as "people who do self-care". That is, we incorporate self-care into our identities. When participants transitioned into someone who does self-care, their self-care practices became more proactive (i.e., not just in response to stress), more regular (e.g., part of their day-to-day lives), and easier for them to do.

Conclusion (TL;DR, But I Hope You Read)

We began this chapter by defining what self-care is and identifying what it is not. We reviewed the history of the term self-care, noted how self-care has been commodified (when it doesn't need to be), and distinguished self-care from soothing. Based on the research we've done in my lab, we define self-care to be anything that *replenishes* you. We spent some time discussing how traditional approaches to self-care get it wrong. We then discussed how to use your core values, identified in the last chapter, to derive workable self-care plans for you. I shared examples from my values of Creating Beauty and Connection. We delved deeper in how to assess the function of behavior to know if it's really self-care, emphasized that there are no right or wrong choices and that instead we must use workability to evaluate our self-care options, and talked about how sometimes self-care doesn't even feel good in the moment. We concluded this chapter by emphasizing that learning what works for you is a process of trial and error.

Notes

1 In the words of Kinsey (2022), "The diet industry is not here to help you. The diet industry is not here to battle some imaginary healthcare crisis. The diet industry is here to take advantage of you and consume your resources. The diet industry commodifies the body and uses it to generate profit" (p. 92).

2 This is not to say that you can't buy things to help with your soothing or self-care. The point is that there are also tools to add to our self-care repertoires that do not cost money, and that we should align our self-care expenditures with our values.

3 I heard 85% of you say, "What time?!?" We'll cover that in the next chapter.

4 But remember, you don't have to do actual running – Winter or otherwise. You're the boss applesauce!

5 Background noise hack: If you are not into golf, golf is a great background noise for working. Shout out to my friend Tim who taught me that.

6 Yes, sometimes I soften and love these activities because they bring us closer together and they love when we do it…. But sometimes I don't soften. I still do the activities because they're values consistent.

7 Except sacrifice implies a value, so let's use choice because it sounds more neutral. There are no right or wrong "sacrifices" just choices that might or might not work for us.

References

Bell, J., Dziekan, G., Pollack, C., & Mahachai, V. (2016). Self-care in the twenty first century: A vital role for the pharmacist, *Advances in Therapy, 33*, 1691–1703. https://doi.org/10.1007/s12325-016-0395-5

Campoli, J., & Cummings, J. A. (2023). "Becoming a values-driven self-care user": Development of a group intervention for health and helping professional students, *Journal of Contextual Behavioral Science, 30*, 191–202. https://doi.org/10.1016/j.jcbs.2023.11.002

Campoli, J., & Cummings, J. A. (2024). "Becoming a person who does self-care": How health care trainees naturalistically develop successful self-care practices. *Journal of Medical Education & Curriculum Development, 11*, 1–11. https://doi.org/10.1177/23821205231223321

Colman, D. E., Echon, R., Lemay, M. S., McDonald, J., Smith, K. R., Spencer, J., & Swift, J. K. (2016). The efficacy of self-care for graduate students in professional psychology: A meta-analysis, *Training and Education in Professional Psychology, 10*, 188–197. https://doi.org/10.1037/tep0000130

Global Wellness Institute. (2023). "Wellness economy statistics & facts." Retrieved January 4, 2023, from https://globalwellnessinstitute.org/press-room/statistics-and-facts/

Kinsey, D. K. (2022). *Decolonizing wellness.* BenBella Books, Inc.

Knowles, L. A., & Cummings, J. A. (2023). Influencers' presentation of self-care on YouTube: It's essential, but inaccessible. *The Journal of Social Media & Society.* In press.

Lakshmin, P. (2023). *Real self-care.* Penguin Random House.

Lorde, A. (2017). *A burst of light and other essays.* Mineola.

School of the Art Institute of Chicago. (n.d.). Retrieved January 26, 2024, from https://libraryguides.saic.edu/learn_unlearn/wellness5#:~:text=The%20Black%20Panther%20Party%20and,as%20it%20was%20and%20is

Chapter 4

Using Values to Guide Your Work and Productivity

Values are not something that we should turn on and off in different contexts. We carry our values with us everywhere; they are part of who we are. Our values can be a vital compass for us to use at work, in addition to guiding our self-care choices. To create a lifestyle that embraces self-care, we need to address our work as well. Containing our work (literally and mentally) creates important space (also literally and mentally) for self-care. Creating a holistic life high in valued living includes more than our careers. Anchoring our work to our values can even help us enjoy our careers. As we discussed at the beginning of this book, working in higher education can be tough. Staying true to our values makes it easier.

There are several features of work in higher education that make values particularly important. One is that there is always more work to be done in academia. I picture our work as a goldfish that will grow to fit whatever living space we provide. Give our goldfish 5 gallons of space, and it will remain relatively small; provide an entire pond, and it will grow much, much bigger. We could work all day, every day, and still have work to do.

There can also be infinite types of work to do. For example, as a faculty member, I have teaching, research, mentoring, service, administrative, and public service tasks, and I can choose (mostly) which ones I want to emphasize on any given day. This involves a lot of decisions to make, which can lead to decision fatigue. This is stressful!

Fortunately, higher education for some workers can also include a fair amount of autonomy, from the way our time is scheduled (or not scheduled) to where we work (since many institutions have now adopted hybrid or remote working options) to the ways we choose to do our work.[1] This autonomy involves a lot of choice. Values can be a great way to guide those choices.

Without a framework to help us decide what to participate in during our academic careers and to guide us to do that in a way that prioritizes our well-being, it is easy to get swept up in a current of saying yes to everything, not structuring our work in the way that works best for us, overworking, and feeling adrift. Values, however, can provide the framework we need.

DOI: 10.4324/9781003379805-5

Staying in Touch With Our Why: Applying Our Values at Work

Just as we used your core value definitions to anchor your self-care plans, we will do the same with values at work. Remember that values can serve as a decision-making tool when we are presented with choices (in our careers and the rest of our lives). This decision-making tool works easier if we know clearly how our values apply to work.

Before we go any further, we must acknowledge that each of us in higher education will have different levels of autonomy and power to dictate our work. As a tenured Full Professor I have a lot more power to structure my days than I did as an untenured Assistant Professor and as precariously employed sessional instructors or graduate students have. This impacts how much flexibility I have in my choices and my ability to set boundaries. I don't want to make it sound like everyone can necessarily find the same amount of flexibility. We want to ask ourselves, "*How* can I do this?" and see what ideas we can generate. But it's not our fault if our position in academia makes our flexibility low.

Just like we did with extrapolating values to our self-care choices, we can also extrapolate them for work. Let's take some time to do that, using the template in Table 4.1. This probably looks familiar, as it's the same strategy we used in the last chapter to brainstorm how to apply our values to self-care.

Table 4.1 Applying Our Values to Work

Core Value	How This Looks at Work

And for an example, here is mine in Table 4.2. You might notice that in this example, I've worked some positive self-statements into my definitions. This helps me remember them!

Table 4.2 Jorden's Values Applied to Work

Core Value	How This Looks at Work
Creating Beauty	Focus on projects and roles that allow me to bring my inquisitive nature and love of learning to my tasks to create beautiful outputs. Use this criteria to evaluate potential projects, tasks, and roles
Connection (Interspecies, Human, Nature)	People are more important than projects. Connect with others and provide support without sacrificing my health. Be generous and ferocious in my protection of those I mentor. Collaborate with fun people.
Being Capable	I have a long history behind me of demonstrating that I can be successful at work, regardless of what is thrown my way. I value security in my job and will seek roles, groups, and tasks that make me feel safe and secure

You can see how in my "Creating Beauty" cell, I've explicitly reminded myself to use this value to help me decide what projects to take on and which to decline (for example, when I am approached as a potential collaborator on something new or asked to participate in a service opportunity).

I've also added a new value to the table, "Being Capable". This value consists of the related values of Adaptability, Conviction, Fortitude, and Security. My definition of this is "Being responsible and capable as I have always been". This reminder ("as I have always been") is my powerful statement to counter the gaslighting I've received as a woman, then non-binary individual, within academia. Often, when those of us who are not WHAMs speak up and challenge "the way it's always been done" (aka the way that has worked for WHAMs), we get met with gaslighting, tone policing, or comments about our "sensitivity". When internalized, these can lead us to doubt ourselves. I remind myself, with my definition, that I am indeed responsible and capable. I remind myself again in my description of how this value translates to my work ("I will seek roles, groups, and tasks that feel safe and secure for me").

I know that I do my best work in groups where I feel safe. Part of being capable at work is allowing myself to decline invitations to work with groups where I don't feel this safety. I used to feel that I should participate in them anyway, as part of my obligation (to whom, exactly? I don't know) to "change the system". I now seek roles, groups, and tasks that feel safe and secure because I know that context will allow me to be as capable as possible and bring my best work to it. In contrast, when I am in groups where I do not feel safe, my capabilities are hindered by the effort I must dedicate to protecting myself from psychological harm.

Understanding our why at work allows us to, first, incorporate our values into what we do – our teaching, mentoring, service, research, administration, and anything else. Second, it provides a compass that allows us to decide what direction we want to move in and, as much as possible, make choices to move toward our values and avoid moving away from them.

A Note on Balancing Obligation with Meaning

Unfortunately, we don't all get 100% choice all of the time in higher education about our work. Depending on our role and our rank, we get more or less autonomy to make these decisions. In other words, we all have obligations as part of our jobs in higher education, with some having more uncontrollable obligations than others. Some of us might be working toward tenure and be obligated to do all the things expected for that, even the parts we don't want to do. Some of us might be teaching more classes than we wish we had to. We might be staff members with less autonomy to choose our specific work tasks. Some of us might be completing degrees and working with advisors we dislike, taking courses we don't see the point in, or working as a teaching assistant when we don't want to.

Should we accept these conditions as "just the way things are"? Absolutely not – and we'll talk about how self-care is an important demonstration of labor activism and a means of pushing back against the oppressive practices of higher education as a system in Chapter 6. At the same time, we often have to do things that we don't want to.

As an example, obtaining tenure as a faculty member involves completing specific work in multiple categories, usually research, teaching, administration/service. Institutions vary in their expectations. For example, while grants are encouraged at my institution, they are not required (as of right now) for tenure. Other institutions require the applicant to have obtained external funding. Certain levels of teaching success might also be expected.

In summary, tenure requirements are not a place in one's career where we can decide what to do or not to do. One cannot obtain tenure by focusing only on one aspect of an institution's requirements and ignoring the others. While some of this work might be consistent with our values, some might not.

Likewise, graduate students might not enjoy or even desire to do all aspects of their graduate training. You might be a staff member who doesn't like your role. That is, there will almost always be aspects of our careers that are obligations and not that which we prefer. I frame the obligations I have to do and can't make values consistent, as the tax I pay for the autonomy to make other tasks as values consistent as possible.

We can try as much as possible to make our work consistent with our values. For example, if we are obligated to be on certain types of committees, we can do our best to choose committees that fit our values (whatever our values might be). If we have to teach specific courses, we can incorporate our values into how we teach them. If we are researchers, we might have the autonomy to choose our program of study. Staff members might be able to choose how to arrange their space or work location to fit their needs best. At the end of the day, there will always be work we do that we don't want to do – but swallowing this pill is easier for me if the rest of my work is as values-consistent as I can make it.

Strategies for Approaching Your Work: How the Rest of this Chapter is Structured

Just like there is no one-size-fits-all approach to self-care and no specific self-care activities that work for everyone, there is no one-size-fits-all way to approach your work either. There is lots and lots of advice for how to work efficiently in higher education. It can be a lot to sift through. The key is allowing your values and how you work best to filter that advice. Finding a workable way to approach your career is a journey of trial and error, just like finding a self-care groove is.

The first part of this chapter focused on defining our core values in the context of work so we understand what aligning our work with our values looks like for us as individuals. In this second part, I will provide some higher-level strategies for you to facilitate your work to make it easier to align with your values, increase your effectiveness, hopefully enjoy it more, and create space for self-care in the "rest of your life". Strategies can help align your work with those values and the definitions you created for them. In this section, I'll provide these strategies, but I am not here to tell you how to do your work. I encourage you to try them and see if they work for you, but not to feel discouraged if you don't like some of them. That's all part of the journey! Likewise, you might already have strategies or learn some from other sources that work great for you.

Overall, I encourage you to be creative when approaching your work. Ask yourself questions such as "Is this working for me?" and "What might make this better for me?" Many of us have more flexibility than we can realize. It can be easy to fall into the trap of "This is how it is done" or to just do what others do without critically evaluating if it works for us.

As someone with multiple chronic illnesses, I have a lot of experience getting creative with how I approach my work. I cannot work the same way every single day – my energy levels can vary daily, and I've learned the hard way that I only feel worse if I don't align my workdays with my energy levels. Sometimes without much warning, I will be ill and need to cancel meetings and adjust my work expectations as needed. We all have different types of days – sometimes, we don't sleep well. We catch illnesses or injure ourselves. Our families need us to care for them, or we have emergencies.

Our aim here is to reflect on our approach to work with two goals: (1) Create more time for self-care and (2) Approach our work so that **the approach becomes self-care in and of itself**. Although we will focus on work in this chapter, there is no reason you can't adopt some of these strategies for any aspect of your life. Remember, you're the boss, applesauce!

I've sorted these strategies into three categories: managing how we approach time, allocating our energy, and developing priorities.

Managing How We Approach Time

If we want to have space for self-care in our lives (both at work and outside of work), then we must make time for self-care. I know that seems like an obvious statement. On one hand, it's simple – allocate some of your time to self-care. Conversely, it's very complicated – because we are all already very busy. Time is a finite resource. **Unless you *actually* allocate some of your time to self-care, it won't happen.**

We've started by stacking the deck in our favor, using self-determination theory and selecting self-care practices that align with our values. This can make it easier to create time for self-care, as we will naturally be more motivated to do values-aligned activities. However, we still need to allocate that time. Time is the number one barrier to self-care, as reported by participants from various career backgrounds, including higher education. We can think of this as a pie chart of 24 hours that we must divide into slices of how we spend that time. **Time is finite; I can only divide my pie by 24 hours**. Thus, a natural consequence is that if I dedicate most of my pie to work, I have less left over for the rest of my life, including self-care. You can see an example in Figure 4.1.

"Why are you starting this section by discussing the ways we think about time?" was a critical (and helpful) question posed by a dear friend who read an early draft of this chapter. I'm glad she asked because it encouraged me to get clearer about my purpose! So here goes:

In higher education, we tend to see time like this: We use our time to produce things. We produce LOTS of different things in higher education: graduates who know things, research papers, grants, policies, tables, spreadsheets, theses, grades, feedback for others, meeting minutes ... I could go on and on. If we want to produce more things, the common wisdom goes, we need to be more efficient with our use of time. Then we will be *faster* at producing things!

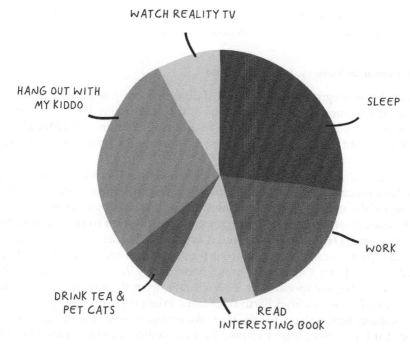

Figure 4.1 Pie chart of time

And that's how we will produce more of them! So, the thinking often goes, if I want to add self-care to my days, then I simply need to become more efficient with my time, accomplish my tasks faster, and then I'll have opened up some time for self-care! Voila!

It can be intuitive to leap into time management strategies and try to be as efficient as humanly possible (or more than humanly possible?) to narrow some of our pie wedges, opening up more pie for other activities. **Higher education adores the idea of becoming more efficient with time to produce more** (as we'll discuss later in this section). As someone who loves time management advice and has spent a lot of time down maximizing efficiency rabbit holes, I can attest that this is a very tempting solution to focus on.

While this approach is valid, to some extent (e.g., if I turn off social media, I sure can write a journal article faster …), **we can only maximize our efficiency so much**. There is a maximum we can maximize. I love efficiency a lot. I am known to be obsessive about reading lifehacks for managing time and experimenting. But there can come a point when this is not workable.

Instead of revamping how we divide our pie, we must first manage our *relationship* with the pie (time). By evaluating how we think, feel, and relate to time, we are setting a base to be critical about how we allocate our time to serve our best interests, both at work and in terms of self-care. Before we change how we allocate our time, we will shine a light on how we think about time so that we can be critical thinkers about our time choices.

Horticultural Time vs. Industrial Time

When I was pregnant with my child, I absorbed every word written by renowned midwife Ina May Gaskin. One of the most lasting lessons I received from her work is not about childbirth or mothering but time. Ina May Gaskin (2003) taught me the difference between horticultural time and industrial time.

Horticultural time is natural time. It's when the sun rises and sets, how long it takes a tomato plant to flower and produce fruit, how long it takes the leaves to fall off the trees in autumn, and how long it takes a baby to be born.

Historically, working in an agrarian economy lent itself to the use of horticultural time (Davies, 2019). However, with the Industrial Revolution and the rise of capitalism came a demand to keep and manage time in a more standardized way. As Jenny Odell notes in her book *Saving Time,* the "origins of the clock, calendar, and spreadsheet are inseparable from the history of extraction, whether of resources from Earth or of labor from people" (2022, p. xvi).

Industrial time is the sixty minutes I take for lunch (some days), the expectation that I work from 9 am to 5 pm, and the number of widgets I might be expected to produce in one hour of factory labor. Industrial time was developed to guarantee raw materials arrived at factories when needed, ensure shifts were worked, and allow trains to arrive and depart in a standardized way (Davies, 2019). Industrial time requires me to have an alarm clock to ensure I'm awake to get myself and my child up and ready to arrive at school in time for the bell that will tell us when the day begins. Table 4.3 demonstrates differences between industrial and horticultural time.

Table 4.3 Industrial Time vs. Horticultural Time

Industrial Time	Horticultural Time
Waking up with an alarm clock	Waking up when our bodies do so on their own
Starting work at 8:30 am every day	Starting work when we feel ready to do so
Writing for 30 mins every day	Writing on days we want to. Write until we feel like stopping

No matter how many clocks, deadlines, and calendars we introduce into our lives, our bodies will still operate on horticultural time. My body decides how much sleep it needs to feel rested. I cannot set an alarm for when my lunch should be digested. There is no set time to recover from COVID-19 if I am unfortunate enough to catch it[2]. What does this mean for approaching our work? It means that we need to balance those parts of being a human that run on horticultural time with those mandated by industrial time. It means when we plan how to divide up our pie of 24 hours, we need to consider what aspects of that plan are influenced by horticultural time.

For example, each morning, I take a medication that almost always upsets my stomach. This medication and its impact on my body does not care what work I have to do during that timeslot – my stomach will be upset regardless. I am somewhat embarrassed to admit that for years I attempted to pay attention to morning meetings while sitting in agonizing physical discomfort because of that medication. Eventually, evaluating whether this was workable for me (it was not), I realized that it might be better if I scheduled different work tasks first thing in the morning that would respect my body, be a little kinder to myself, and allow me to get some work done. Now, I spend that chunk of time writing. As much as possible, I also work at home for that time as I'm more physically comfortable with an upset stomach at home than on campus.

In Table 4.4, I encourage you to note any places in your life where you notice experiences influenced by horticultural time (or maybe conflicts between horticultural and industrial time in your days). While I've given you space to brainstorm some ways to honor these needs, if you don't have any ideas right now about how to do that, it's perfectly fine.

Table 4.4 Your Horticultural Time Needs and Ways to Meet Them

Horticultural Time Needs	Ways to Meet Them

Remember: Maximizing Efficiency is a Task of Late-Stage Capitalism

Core to capitalism is never-ending growth (i.e., making money) … and constantly growing (i.e., improving) despite each day only holding 24 hours. "In the drive to make time equal more money", notes Odell (2023 p. 25), "the employer has two strategies to pursue: extension (increasing the amount of time that money buys) or intensification (demanding more work for the same amount of time)". Suppose we were working in factories in the 1910s. In that case, we might have seen scientists and researchers observing and tweaking our work environment to increase productivity (and thus profit extraction): turning the lights brighter or dimmer and making the assembly line faster to increase the number of widgets made in the same amount of time. Minimizing the steps workers need to take from workstation to workstation. This is Taylorism (or "Scientific Management"), and it's still in use today (Scientific Management, 2023).

In higher education, we see clear evidence of extension and intensification. Hiring sessional instructors who cost the institution less and are given many more classes to teach than a tenured faculty member. Increasing expectations around how many papers, books, and grants faculty should be producing each year. Mandating that graduate students serve as teaching assistants for below-poverty wages. Reducing the number of administrative workers while expecting the remaining workers to produce the same quantity of output. These are just some examples of how higher education works to generate more capital from its employees.

While it is helpful to consider time management, we also need to know where this drive comes from and who benefits from it. We need to be careful to always consider workability as a filter through which we evaluate any strategies designed to improve the efficiency of our use of time. We must ask ourselves, "Is this a strategy that makes my job more *workable for me*?" If the answer is no, we shouldn't bother using it.

Too often, strategies for how to use our time more efficiently are framed solely as ways to make us more productive (i.e., to grind the gears of capitalism) for the ultimate benefit of our employer. Likewise, even leisure time (e.g., self-care) is often sold to us as a strategy to make us more productive at work (Odell, 2023). Said differently, and frankly, I don't care if you are more productive for your employer. What I care about is your well-being. **The only strategies worth adopting are the ones that are workable for you and improve your quality of life.** There is no point in being productive for productivity's sake. This book is not about using self-care to achieve more or to be more productive. It's about using self-care to create a wonderful life worth living that feels vibrant and full.

How We Use Our Time is Morally Neutral

Existing in concert with the idea that we should maximize our efficiency to become as productive as possible is the idea that productivity is a moral virtue. Odell notes, "[p]articularly in the United States, it's not just busyness that's considered good – its a specific image of industry, the result of a long romance among morality, self-improvement, and capitalist business principles" (Odell, 2023, p. 44) and "we are taught from the beginning that faithfully squeezing the most value out of your twenty-four hours … is what a good person does" (Odell, 2023, p. 75).

The correlation between productivity and virtue is a message that higher education also loves. We praise people who go above and beyond and give merit raises to those who publish the most. We share horror stories of our sleep deprivation that are silently competition for who is working the hardest. We beat ourselves up and feel like bad people when we "waste time",[3] or don't write every day or take too long to answer emails (or don't answer emails at all). Underneath all this messaging is the idea that good people accomplish a lot and bad people are lazy and produce hardly anything (in higher education, we call those professors "dead wood").

However, the reality is that how we use our time (in self-care, leisure, and work) is morally neutral. Likewise, the speed at which you do any activity is morally neutral. All that matters is if you're using your time in a workable (for you) way to achieve your goals and move toward your values. Writing a grant versus answering emails versus watching television versus eating cake versus analyzing data…. None of these uses of time is any better than the others.

We Do Not All Have the Same 24 Hours Each Day

In her book, Odell also reminds us that the idea that we "all have the same 24 hours" is false and inaccurate. It is another assumption that capitalism wants us to internalize so that we will focus on producing as much as possible. I will add discriminatory to the list as well. Odell discusses the work of others who also label this for the ableism that it is.

For example, as someone with a chronic illness, I spend more time at medical appointments than colleagues without such an illness. To manage my chronic pain, I ideally incorporate physiotherapy exercises and stretching into each day, attend regular massage, myofascial release, and dry needling appointments. I get ten hours of sleep every night to be at my best. I have a young child who I spend time with, who needs lunches made and laundry done. Everyone's 24 hours look different.

Time is Limited, But Not Scarce

Time is indeed limited – we cannot create more of it, and when a moment has passed, it is gone forever. But time is not necessarily scarce. Almost all of us have *enough* time. For example, I hear a lot of professors (including myself) despair, "How will I get all of these things done?" but for the most part … everything that needs to get done gets done. (And if we change our minds and decide not to do something, that's often a workable choice).

Horticultural time is illustrated each summer when I plant my garden. My favorite vegetable to grow, by far, is cherry tomatoes. I adore cherry tomatoes – the colors they come in, the flavors, and the various sizes. I plant marigolds around them to distract pests and basil as a soil buddy. When I plant my baby tomatoes, often from seedlings I begin myself, I don't know exactly how many days it will take them to grow tall, flower, or produce fruit. I could not tell you the date those tomatoes will be ripe enough to eat. However, I know that nature will do her thing, and eventually, I will be roasting tomatoes, popping them in salads, and eating them directly off the vine in my backyard. It will take the amount of time it takes. The tomatoes have *enough* time. They have precisely the amount of time they need.

Higher education, with its neoliberal values, frames time as scarce. When we see time that way – and experience the associated fear that comes along anytime our brains perceive scarcity – we will try to use our time as efficiently as possible to maximize our output. If time at work feels scarce, we will be much more likely to use that "extra" ninety minutes in our evenings on work instead of self-care.

Okay, You Can Divide up That Pie Now ... with a Caveat[4]

Here is the moment that some of you have been awaiting! Dividing up our time pie to match our needs and work tasks. You now have the tools to be critical about allocating your time. That is you:

- Know that you exist in both horticultural time and industrial time, and there are sometimes conflicts between them.
- Understand that the pull to maximize efficiency is a characteristic of extractive capitalism, and there is a maximum we can maximize.
- Know that how you allocate time is morally neutral.
- Understand that we don't all have the same 24 hours in a day.
- And respect time for being limited but not scarce.

And you know that it is essential to ask yourself, "Is this workable for me?" in as many of your time choices as possible and work hard to make them workable.

But … here comes the caveat. Even if we don't all have the *same 24 hours* in our days, we each only have 24 hours. We cannot allocate more than 24 hours. And if you want some of those hours to include self-care, you must allocate them there.

Allocating Our Energy

Energy is often an overlooked personal resource in higher education. Our attention is often focused on time. Energy and time are often conflated. As someone with what feels like a permanent energy deficit, I can assure you they are not. Whereas time refers to those hours on the clock carved out by industrial time, energy refers to how much capacity we have. Managing and allocating our energy is an important strategy for bringing our values to work (ideally making sure we have energy for those values-consistent things we love to do in our careers) and making sure that we have energy left over for self-care and creating a life worth living outside of our careers as well.

Biological Prime Time

I'm writing this section on an autumn Sunday morning[5]. The sky is a bright blue with wispy white clouds lazily floating along (on horticultural time). Yellow elm leaves are falling from the trees in my neighborhood. I'm drinking an eggnog latte and still in my pajamas. I rolled out of bed, to the coffee maker, to my desk. And I like it this way. Why? Because the morning, right after I wake up, is my biological prime time.

Biological Prime Time is a concept I first learned about from Chris Bailey, author of *The Productivity Project* (2016). Everyone's energy goes up and down during the day. Of course, our energy will be impacted by all kinds of variables: how much sleep you got, if you've had any caffeine, if you have a chronic illness, or even if your brain feels like focusing on any given day. The idea behind Biological Prime Time is that there are times of the day for each of us when our energy is (predictably) higher than others. As I mentioned, for me, this is right after I wake up in the morning. In *The Productivity Project*, Chris mentions that his biological prime time is between 10 am to noon and 5 pm to 8 pm. Conversely, we also have times of the day when our energy is low. For me, this tends to be around 12 pm to 2 pm and after 4 pm, when my brain is usually out of energy to focus on work.

Understanding your biological prime time can be a fantastic strategy for allocating your energy throughout the day. We can match our work tasks to the levels of energy that we have over the day. For example, biological prime time can be a great time of the day to do work tasks that require creativity, focus, and a lot of attention. This is why I love days when I can use my biological prime time for writing.[6] In contrast, I use my naturally low-energy parts of the day for tasks that don't require as much creativity or deep focus, like meetings, reconciling my purchasing card, or tidying up my office.

Matching our work to our energy is a powerful act of self-compassion and self-care in and of itself. For example, forcing my mind and body to try to write at my lowest energy time of the day is an exercise in frustrating, unkind futility. My brain will not produce the words I want it to (because it is tired) – and why would I treat my brain that way?

Our energy also wavers across days, weeks, and months. We are not widget machines that can produce the same number and quality of widgets daily, month after month. We are human beings, and human beings run on horticultural time. Thus, it is also an act of self-care (and productivity) to accept that our energy will wax and wane across seasons and to try to match our use of biological prime time to these changes.

Selective Perfectionism

Many of us in higher education bring our maximum capacity to every task we do. Higher education certainly encourages us to do so. There are three issues with this tendency, however. First, bringing 100% (or 110%!) of our capacity to every single aspect of our careers in higher education is a recipe for exhaustion and burnout. We cannot do everything expected of us at that level of commitment. Second, doing everything perfectly takes a lot of time and energy – probably more than full time in any given week. By spending all our energy on ensuring everything at work is done perfectly, we will leave ourselves with little time for anything else, including self-care. Last, working at 100% or 110% of our capacity leaves no room for flexibility or changes in our capacity, or variations in how much effort is required to bring 100% to everything (Norcross & Guy, 2007). For example, sometimes we get sick, have caregiving responsibilities, or sometimes unexpected tasks arise. If we are already at our total capacity when those unexpected things arise, we have less flexibility or energy to deal with them.

One solution to this dilemma is a skill I love called selective perfectionism. I cannot take credit for this skill; it's outlined by Julie Morgenstern in her book *Time to Parent* (2018). Selective perfectionism means deciding, preferably ahead of time, how much of our capacity, energy, and striving to do perfect work we will bring to our tasks. There are three levels of selective perfectionism: minimum (MIN), moderate (MOD), and maximum (MAX). Deciding ahead of time which responsibilities and tasks are worthy of MAX and which can be MINed (and then sticking to that decision!) is an effective way of managing our energy. It can also help us be values-consistent at work and manage our obligation versus meaning balancing by permitting ourselves to bring our full capacity to some tasks (ideally the values-consistent ones) and less of our capacity to others (ideally the values-inconsistent ones).

I want to take a moment to respond to some of you who might be thinking, "I can't do a shitty job on my work!" and note that allotting minimum capacity is not the same as doing a shitty, irresponsible job (although it could be if you decide that's what MIN means – you're the boss here too, applesauce). For many of us, our minimum capacity is still pretty fantastic work.

The way I use selective perfectionism is to assign to each semester's tasks (which I know ahead of time because I use the National Center for Faculty Development & Diversity's Semester Plan approach – strongly recommend because the more we can plan ahead of time, the more that plan can incorporate self-care and the more we stack the deck in our favor that we will actually do it).

After I've created my Semester Plan, I go through and decide which tasks I will assign MIN (minimum), MOD (moderate), or MAX (maximum) levels of perfectionism (and thus energy) to. You can see an example of this in Table 4.5. There are some tasks (like manuscripts) that I know I will be unable to avoid bringing MAX to, so I go ahead and assign MAX where I know I won't be able to resist.[7] I try to be aware that I cannot MAX everything and limit myself to 1-2 MAX activities per semester.

Some semesters, I am aware I don't have the capacity I usually do, often due to my chronic illness or parenting responsibilities, so I might not have any MAX tasks. I also make sure to take the time to define what MIN, MOD, and MAX mean for

Table 4.5 Jorden's Example Definitions of MIN, MOD, and MAX

Task	MIN	MOD	MAX
Teaching	I will teach this course following the syllabus I have already prepared. I will not update or re-develop any aspects of this class	I will primarily teach this course the way it is already prepared, but I will update some course materials and/or assignments that could be of better quality or more efficient for me as the instructor	This course is new to me or needs a full redevelopment and/or update of the course materials or I have created assignments that need labor-intensive mentoring from me as the instructor.
Committee Work	I will attend meetings and share my thoughts and opinions. I will not join any subcommittees and I will minimize the work required of me between meetings	I will attend meetings and share my thoughts. I will consider joining a subcommittee or volunteering to assist in a minimal way (like taking minutes)	I will volunteer to chair this committee or a subcommittee. I will complete work related to this committee between meeting times
Research	This semester I will continue to revise manuscripts and work on my data backlog. I will not start any new projects	I will work on projects that require design and/or data analysis. I will not engage in any projects that require learning new literature or new skills	I will begin a research project and/or grant application in an area that will require an extensive literature review from me and/or new skills

each task. Because if we don't know what exactly what we mean by MIN, MOD, and MAX, it is easy for all of them just to become MAX. The clearer we can be with ourselves, the more we can hold ourselves accountable for the commitment we made. And, don't forget – what you MIN, MOD, or MAX is morally neutral. There is no virtue in MAXing everything nor sin in MINing it all either!

My definitions might change from semester to semester. Note that just like self-care, there are no right or wrong definitions here, only workable ones for you. You do not have to copy or even like my definitions. Instead, you should find the ones that work for you.

Procrastination as a Message from Your Intuition

One of my strategies for keeping myself organized at work is to do a weekly brain dump. I get out a blank piece of paper, and I write down all of the things rattling around in my brain that have to be done – either imminently or some-day. I grab it all from my mind and get it written down. Then I go through my email and pull out all the tasks in my inbox that need to be done. I copy-forward any items from my brain dump the week before. I get all the "to dos" out on paper, no matter how far away the due date is for that task. This means "answer that email from so-and-so", "plan a summer vacation", and anything in between might appear on my list.

Often, surprise, surprise, the same tasks come up over and over again. And over again. And over again … you get the drift. I don't think I am alone in this, but I have sometimes carried tasks **across an entire semester of brain dumps** and still not done them.

It is easy for me to feel shame about this. It's easy to internalize blame for these things we never get to. But what if there was another way to frame pro-crastination? What if procrastination was – hear me out – your brain telling you that you shouldn't be doing the work you're not doing? That's so impor-tant, I will repeat it: **What if "procrastination" is your brain telling you that you shouldn't be doing that task?**

What if what we frame as procrastination is actually intuition? (LaPorte, 2012). In her book *The Firestarter Sessions,* Danielle LaPorte argues that "what seems like avoidance may be a deeper inkling of wrong timing" (p. 48). Our procrastination might be our mind and intuition telling us that this work is not for us – and that's okay. How much of your procrasti-nation is, for example, working with colleagues that drag you down? What if you're avoiding writing that paper because you're just not that into it? Or you're not getting that policy drafted because you don't agree with the policy at all?

In her work, LaPorte connects this dismissing of intuition as procrastination wrapped up in what she calls the "myth of endurance" (p. 44). According to the myth of endurance, work is supposed to be hard. We're supposed to push ourselves, "pay your dues. Put in your time. Prove yourself … stay the course. Meet expectations" (LaPorte, 2012, p. 44).

In contrast, we are allowed to make our work easy. As LaPorte so elegantly says,

> Choosing easy is smart, efficient, elegant; a fantastic form of self-compassion; giving yourself a break and getting out of your own way. Choosing easy is letting inspiration be your compass. Choosing easy is allowing for the things that you've been asking for to enter your life.
>
> (2012, p. 44).

Now, I hear some of you saying, "Okay, but…. I can't just do only what I want to Jorden. I have obligations to fulfill!"

I hear you but … hear me out. So much of life in higher education, for many of us, is indeed within our control. (And if it's not in our control yet, it might be as we progress in our career.) I need to do research, but I decide what topic I research. I need to teach, but I decide how I teach. I need to do service, but I choose which activities to say yes to and which to say no to. I need to do my job, but I decide how much perfectionism to bring to each career domain.[8]

LaPorte clarifies between two types of easy: quality easy and cheap easy. Quality easy "has a sense of fluidity to it. There's a gravitational pull *forward*. Quality easy relies on his inner strength. Quality easy has an abiding respect for herself" (2012, p. 44).

Quality easy is the type of easy that says, "Oh my god, I am going to design this research study because I *have to know* the answer to this research question!" It's the kind of easy that says "You know, I'm going to revise that assignment for my undergraduates so it links the learning objectives a bit more tightly to their lived experience". It's the easy that we sit down and feel compelled to do.

Cheap easy is

> a sucker for a discount. Cheap easy can't see that some losses are gains. Cheap easy stays in a stifling relationship because it seems easier than facing the heartbreak and dividing up the furniture. Cheap easy is frequently in a rush, a smidge desperate, and usually scrambling for options.
>
> (LaPorte, 2012, p. 45).

Cheap easy stays on an academic committee that makes us want to cry and pull our hair out or leads us to a glass of wine afterward to cope. Cheap easy is grinding through teaching a class in a way that we hate because "that's how other people do it".

What does this have to do with allocating our energy? In my experience, **cheap easy is wildly inefficient with energy**. It takes me so much longer to complete a task that I hate or am "procrastinating" on than choosing quality easy. So why not choose it?

Developing Priorities

If there is one constant truth of higher education, no matter your specific role, there is always more work to be done. If you try to do it all right now, you will exhaust yourself (and probably be wildly inefficient and accomplish very little of it, too). I'm speaking from personal experience!

To thrive in higher education in a way that supports our well-being at work and in our self-care, we need to make choices. We need to have priorities. If you don't make your priorities, then you are likely to be swept along in someone else's. Or you'll say yes to everything, like I did in my first semester on the tenure track.

Our values are a great place to begin developing priorities. As referenced earlier in this chapter, some of my core values are creativity, connection, and being capable. As a reminder, here in Table 4.6 how I define those values and apply them specifically to my career:

Table 4.6 Jorden's Values & Definitions for Work

Core Value	How This Looks at Work
Creating Beauty	Focus on projects and roles that allow me to bring my inquisitive nature and love of learning to my tasks to create beautiful outputs. Use this criteria to evaluate potential projects, tasks, and roles
Connection (Interspecies, Human, Nature)	People are more important than projects. Connect with others and provide support without sacrificing my health. Be generous and ferocious in my protection of those I mentor. Collaborate with fun people
Being Capable	I have a long history behind me of demonstrating that I can be successful at work, regardless of what is thrown my way. I value security in my job and will seek roles, groups, and tasks that make me feel safe and secure

While these values assist me with deciding how to allocate my time and what to focus on, I still have many more opportunities than hours in the day. That is, I still need to decide what my priorities are.

Priorities don't need to stay the same forever. Just as different seasons of our lives require us to prioritize different values, there are different seasons of our careers. In the National Center for Faculty Development and Diversity Faculty Success Program, Kerry Ann Roquemore conceptualizes our career as a "book of many chapters", each of which will likely have a different focus.

How Do You Want to Feel in Your Career?

Working in higher education trains us to focus on accomplishments. What's the next thing we need to get done? What is the next goal we need to cross off of our list? Sometimes I think working in academia has made me so focused on achievements that it's difficult to stop and savor them when they come. There is always some next level to be striving toward.

However, accomplishments are not the only metric for defining success. What if there was another way to approach your career? To that end, consider how you want to *feel* in your career. As Danielle LaPorte notes, "knowing how you actually want to feel is the most potent form of clarity that you can have. Generating those feelings is the most creative thing you can do with your life" (2012, pp. 62–63). Instead of deciding first what we want to achieve, we can decide how we want to feel and use this as a guide for what to do.

We can derive some of these intentional feelings from our core values by reflecting on what living those values at work feels like. For example, Table 4.7 shows some feelings that I associate with my three core values I described earlier:

Table 4.7 Jorden's Values and Associated Feelings

Core Value	Associated Feelings
Creating Beauty	Inspired
	Motivated
	Curious
Connection (Interspecies, Human, & Nature)	Excited
	Bonded
	Understood
	Authentic

(Continued)

Table 4.7 (Continued)

Core Value	Associated Feelings
Being Capable	Calm
	Confident
	Able

Knowing how I want to *feel* in my career helps me decide what tasks and activities to prioritize. I can seek research projects I am genuinely curious about and inspired/motivated to finish. I work on research questions that I burn for answers to. I seek collaborations with others who excite me, with people I feel understand me, share my passions, and allow me to be authentic. I engage in service and administrative activities where my skills can shine and feel calm and confident. When I feel these ways, I do my best work.

I'm also aware of how I don't want to feel at work based (unfortunately) on many years of feeling that way: Anxious, critiqued, psychologically unsafe, inferior, judged, inadequate, awkward, broken, inappropriate, "too sensitive". Not surprisingly, I don't do my best work in these feeling states. The mental health and physical health concerns they trigger also interfere with me engaging in self-care and living my best life. For too long in my career, I stayed in professional situations that evoked these feelings, thinking that it was "just how things are" or that I needed to fight to change the system. We'll talk more about this in the next chapter. For now, remember, we don't have to engage in the myth of endurance (LaPorte, 2012); we can choose quality easy.

What Are Your Essential Career Goals (for This Season)?

Deciding our priorities includes deciding what to focus on (and what not to focus on) in any given season of our lives and careers.

"Eighty percent of your to do list is crap", says Brigid Schulte in her book *Overwhelmed: Work, Love, and Play When No One Has the Time* (2014). "Look, the stuff of life never ends. That is life … So you have to decide. What do you want to accomplish in this life? What's *important* to you right now?" (Schulte, 2014, p. 256). What's important is personal – only you can decide what to focus on right now. What to focus on should be decided with your values and related goals in mind.

One challenge of the open-ended nature of work in higher education, combined with the never-ending work to be done, is deciding where to focus at any given time. The "disciplined pursuit of less" (p. 5) is the entire focus of

Greg McKeown's *Essentialism* (2014). As McKeown outlines, Essentialists discern what is truly important at any given time, say no to what is not, and "get the right things done" (2014, p. 8). How do we decide what the "right" things are at any given time? By using our values and goals. For example, if you are a graduate student then you might decide what is essential to you is focusing on anything that brings you closer to graduating. If you are a tenure-track new assistant professor, it might be your tenure and promotion requirements. You might also decide that what is essential is something besides work, like me picking my kiddo up from school every day or having time to get enough sleep. No one can tell you what's essential in any given season of your life.

No Lists & N-Committees

No Lists and N-Committees can be tremendous resources for setting work boundaries around things that we don't want to do (or maybe want to do but shouldn't do at this exact time). They are especially nice after you've planned out your semester and figured out your MIN, MOD, and MAX definitions and allocations to go with what you'll be focusing on (i.e., your essentials). Just as important as deciding what we will be doing at work is actively deciding what we will *not* be doing.

No Lists are exactly what they sound like. It's a list of things that you will be striving not to do at any given time. One of the exciting parts of working in higher education is that a lot of opportunities come our way: new classes and new students, new tasks, new collaborations. These opportunities can also be a curse, especially because higher education loves to send us messages about scarcity, which can lead us to think that if we say no to an opportunity, it will never come our way again. This thought can be a slippery slope to overwork.

There are lots of different ways to structure a no list. Here are some examples I've seen:

- I will not take on any new course preps this year or revise any of my syllabi.
- I will review 2 manuscripts for every 1 manuscript that I submit.
- I will review 5 manuscripts this year.
- I will not be on more than 10 dissertation committees at any given time.
- I will not respond to emails outside of business hours.
- I will decline any invitations to join new collaborations this year.
- I will not write any grants this semester, no matter how enticing they seem.
- I will take my lunch hour instead of working.
- I will not have more than 5 graduate students in my lab at any given time.

No Lists encourage us to complement our decisions of what we will focus on with the things we plan to set aside for a given amount of time. As you can see from some of the examples on this list, you might pick a number of any given requests to say yes to, and then say no after that (e.g., the number of manuscript reviews you will do in one year).

Your own No List should consider all of the concepts we've discussed in this chapter, like your views on time, your level of energy, and definitely what your essential priorities are in any given season of your career. And just like how we decide to use our time is morally neutral, so is deciding how not to use our time! You can adjust your no-list with each new semester, year, or career chapter (or whatever time frame works best for you).

Even with our MIN/MOD/MAX definitions and our No List of what we will avoid, it can still be difficult to say no. Or, sometimes opportunities come along that really do seem like they might be a good idea to alter our plans for.[9]

In this situation, what can be helpful is an N-Committee (N stands for No!). Your N-Committee is another person, or a group of people, who will evaluate opportunities and help you decide what to do. Note that it is labeled an N-Committee because **the default answer from this committee is always a hard no.** It should take a lot of convincing for your N-Committee to decide that you should say yes to something. And if N-Committee does agree you should do something, the very next question N-Committee is supposed to ask you is, "What are you going to give up, to make space for this new thing?"

When deciding who to choose for your N-Committee, you want to choose people who cannot be easily swayed and who will be ruthless with their No[10]. And then you want to appreciate the heck out of them because it's not easy to be an N-Committee member. You might even want to consider trading services and being a member of their N-Committee too. Last, it will be important to get into the habit of consulting with N-committee about new opportunities you have. One way to get into this habit is to schedule regular N-committee time (e.g., at the start of a new semester, monthly, or whatever interval works for you). With the use of an N-Committee over time, you will likely find that you internalize the ideas of N-Committee. For example, knowing my N-Committee well means knowing what they will likely say. As a result, I say no to more things on my own now without needing to go to them.

Placing Workability at the Center of Any Plan

This chapter has included some specific systems and processes to help you apply your values to your work. I want to end this chapter by emphasizing that you don't have to use or even like these systems – remember that the key is what works for YOU. Don't bother with it if it's not workable for you!

Figure 4.2 There were a lot of options in this chapter to try – you got this!

Photo by Sydney Rae, available on Unsplash at https://unsplash.com/photos/brown-dried-leaves-on-sand-geM5lzDj4lw

Conclusion (TL;DR, But I Hope You Read)

Not only are values useful for guiding our self-care, but they can help us approach our work as well. We can use our values to reduce work to create more time and space for self-care and we can, ideally, approach our work in a way that is in and of itself self-care. I began this chapter by demonstrating how to define our values for work. I touched on balancing obligation work with more meaningful work that matches our values. Regarding more specific work strategies, we discussed managing how we approach time, allocating our energy, the role of "procrastination" in our intuition, and developing work priorities. I concluded by reminding readers to place workability at the center of any plan.

Notes

1 It is important, however, to acknowledge that not all workers in higher education will experience this type of autonomy, particularly staff.
2 Unfortunately, as someone with a questionable immune system, I caught multiple illnesses while writing this book, including COVID-19 twice. Once I tested positive for 21 days. The other for 8 days. This is definitely horticultural time. However, my health region says that I only need to stay home for 5 days if I catch COVID-19, which is an application of industrial time (to an infectious disease).

3 Are we wasting time or does our body, which runs on horticultural time, need a break?
4 This is somewhat figurative because you should probably finish this chapter before you do that though.
5 Reminder that no one is requiring you to work weekends. (I usually don't). Working weekends or not is morally neutral.
6 Can I use every day's biological prime time for writing? Nope. I naturally have to spend some of my biological prime time getting myself and my kiddo awake, ready for the day, and off to school. Remember we're not aiming for perfection here, we're aiming for workability and a fit with your actual life.
7 That is, it would take more energy for me to resist MAXing my writing, so I choose instead to just allocate my energy to MAX there. But you don't have to decide to do what I do!
8 I again acknowledge that how much autonomy we have varies. While not every avenue of control might be open to you in your work, my guess is that you do have some autonomy in some places.
9 If you change your semester plan to add something impromptu, you also need to remove something else.
10 I am not always a ruthless N-Committee member, so I try to speak in the third person and distance myself (Jorden) from my role as an N-Committee member. For example, I will say to someone, "Well, N-Committee does not think that this is a good idea" because I can be more certain than if I use the first person.

References

Bailey, C. (2016). *The productivity project*. Random House Canada.
Davies, A. C. (2019). *The industrial revolution and time*. The Open University. Retrieved January 26, 2024, from https://www.open.edu/openlearn/history-the-arts/history-science-technology-medicine/the-industrial-revolution-and-time
Gaskin, I. M. (2003). *Ina May's guide to childbirth*. Bantam.
LaPorte, D. (2012). *The fire starter sessions: A soulful + practical guide to creating success on your own terms*. Harmony.
McKeown, G. (2014). *Essentialism*. Crown Business.
Morgenstern, J. (2018). *Time to parent: Organizing your life to bring out the best in your child and you*. Holt Paperbacks.
Norcross, J. C., & Guy, J. D. Jr (2007). *Leaving it at the office: A guide to psychotherapist self-care*. Guilford.
Odell, J. (2023). *Saving time: Discovering a life beyond the clock*. Random House.
Schulte, B. (2014). *Overwhelmed: Work, love, and play when no one has the time*. Harper Perennial.
Scientific management. (2023, December 20). In *Wikipedia*. Retrieved January 26, 2024, from https://en.wikipedia.org/wiki/Scientific_management

Chapter 5

The Dark Side of Values at Work

More and more, I see businesses that place their core values front and center on their promotional materials, self-help books that place values as central to their recommendations, and people researching the importance of values in our careers. However, values have a dark side. Our values can be unhelpful if we take extreme measures to pursue them or don't keep them within the realm of personal workability. Our values can also make us vulnerable to exploitation by others, including our institutions. In this chapter, we will discuss some examples of how our values can pull us (or our institutions can capitalize on our values to pull us) into unworkable situations and how to navigate to workability. We'll also talk about letting go of changing others and the sole purpose of a job (Spoiler Alert: It is not to make you feel fulfilled).

Taking Pursuing Our Values to Unhelpful Extremes

Living a life consistent with your values is good. Pursuing them using extreme measures and without flexibility is not. We need to pursue valued living with workability in mind. That is, pursuing our values in ways that are not workable for us is not helpful.

For example, in Chapter 4, we discussed how higher education loves to send us messages about being more productive, and this includes lots of hacks and advice for how to use our time more efficiently. I mentioned how easy it can be to pursue maximum efficiency. It can be easy to buy into self-improvement hype and constantly focus on improving who we are (and thus never settling into who we are). For example, as previously discussed, we can take life and efficiency hacks a little too far – and the narrative of self-improvement "promises us that someday we can reach a pinnacle of productivity and efficiency such that our life will finally feel like it's fully under control" (Lakshim, 2023, p. 35).

DOI: 10.4324/9781003379805-6

We can quickly lose sight, when immersed in productivity hacks, of the fact that there is more to life than producing and that our bodies work on horticultural time. We are not computers who always act and produce the same if given the same inputs. It is possible to become so focused on efficient accomplishment that we don't pause to ask ourselves why we are doing the tasks we are doing or if the productivity strategy is workable for us. Moreover, for a lot of us in higher education, our careers require us to have time to think, percolate, and ponder. From the outside (to extractive capitalism), these tasks can look inefficient, and we can internalize this idea; however, they are core to producing great work.

More than one productivity- or efficiency-based advice author has revised their perspective. This includes Chris Bailey, author of *The Productivity Project* (2016), who went on to write *How to Calm Your Mind* (2022) after his own experience with burnout and anxiety. This doesn't mean, as Bailey notes, that we throw the baby of productivity out with the bathwater. We just need to be aware of when our approaches are helpful versus not helpful for us.

Some of the most challenging values to balance with workability are those related to helping and giving to others. This can be particularly challenging for higher education workers because most of us have others who rely upon our work – be it students who need us to grade assignments, coauthors who need us to write, faculty who need us to help maintain policies and support their work, or advisors who want us to complete our dissertation on time. And, as already mentioned, there is always more work to be done. In other words, more people are always relying on us.

If you have a core personal value related to supporting others, it can feel impossible to set boundaries around giving even when that giving is no longer workable for you. For example, I know many faculty members who have been unable to fully take their well-deserved vacation time or even their parental leave because there are no backup plans to ensure their students are still supported in making progress in their research work. I know staff who always pause their work to help others, even when extremely burnt out. Arguably, in this situation, the behaviors being driven by our values are no longer workable for us.

The Joys and Dangers of Having a Calling

Many people in higher education see their careers as more than a job. Those of us in academia can wrap our identities up in our jobs, sometimes at the expense of living a full life that involves interests and experiences outside of work. Some higher education workers feel that their career is a calling, a passion, or what they have been "meant to do" with their lives. That is, people with a calling see their work as more than a way to receive income. For them, it is also an opportunity to find meaning and to make a difference in the world (Cardador & Caza, 2012). A substantial body of research shows the benefits of having a calling. People who work in a career consistent with their calling experience more career satisfaction and less intention of quitting (Gazica & Spector, 2015), and even more life satisfaction (Duffy, Allan, Autin, & Bott, 2013). Reaping these benefits is great … if it is workable for you. Employees who perceive themselves as having a calling can be great for employers, too. For example, these employees tend to be more committed to their organizations and have higher performance levels (Rawat & Nadavulakere, 2015).

However, there are downsides to having a calling – especially if you are in a career that doesn't allow you to pursue that calling or a job that doesn't provide the appropriate resources. More examples of negative outcomes include "developing career tunnel vision" (Cardador & Caza, 2012, p. 339) and giving an unworkable amount of personal sacrifice to pursue the calling, including at the expense of other parts of one's life. Studies of nurses and teachers have shown that the benefits of pursuing a calling wane over longer careers (Cardador & Caza, 2012), a concept that Hartnett and Kline (2005) termed a "fall from the call" (p. 19). Not having a calling at all is better for our health than an unanswered one (Gazica & Spector, 2015).

The narrative of being fortunate to pursue our passion as a career is "deeply romanticized" (Kim, Campbell, Shepherd, & Kay, 2019, p. 1), including in higher education. People who work in higher education are often touted for being able to pursue their passion, which is often one reason why working in higher education is marketed as desirable (e.g., Edwards, 2013; Honor Society, 2023).

There is evidence that being able to pursue a passion in our career choices is a positive thing. For example, passion for work is related to life satisfaction and our subjective feelings of happiness for both general workers (Yukhymenko-Lescroart & Sharma, 2020) and academic faculty (Yukhymenko-Lescroart & Sharma, 2019). Students' passion for education is related to dedication, persistence, engagement, and creativity (Ruiz-Alfonso & León, 2016). Passion is associated with positive group interactions and decreased conflict, and workers report that not having passion at work can result in work losing meaning (Kim et al., 2019). However, having a calling can also set us up for some negative experiences. For example, passion can lead to burnout (Vallerand, Paquet, Phillippe, & Charest, 2010).

Our values have a soft underbelly at work: They can leave us vulnerable to exploitation by the neoliberal-obsessed, "do more with less" capitalist system of higher education.

When we think "exploitation at work", what might be more likely to come to mind are extreme examples from other industries, like child labor practices, physically dangerous working conditions, or exporting work to developing countries to pay poverty wages (Kim et al., 2019). As Kim and colleagues note, other forms of exploitation might fly under our radar, "such as pressuring employees to work extra hours for no pay, to sacrifice family time for work, or to engage in undesirable tasks that are irrelevant to their job description" (p. 1). Sound familiar?

Kim and colleagues (2019) describe that passion can be used to "legitimize and justify potentially exploitative managerial practices (p. 2), a process they refer to as passion exploitation. They note that what makes these practices particularly unfair (and thus exploitative) are the lack of additional pay or benefits for the employees asked to do additional work, the possibility of some of the work being demeaning, and when workers do not benefit from the additional work. Moreover, employees are "unlikely…[to] feel completely free to decline these requests" (p. 2) because of the power differentials between themselves and their employers. This can occur in higher education, for example, when contingent or precariously employed instructors are asked to do more work than paid for, often with the implication that doing this additional work will lead to a department or institution being more likely to renew their precarious contract or not doing the work will lead to students suffering. It can occur when junior untenured professors are pressured to do additional service work – particularly those from minority groups. Last, an entirely separate book could be written about how passion exploitation is used to suppress graduate student wages and exploit trainees in the name of "preparing them for their careers". This path from having a calling, to giving more than we have, to exploitation, to burnout is illustrated in Figure 5.1.

One example, more directly tied to values that often play out in academia, is the exploitation of values related to community, conscientiousness, "the better good", and contribution. People take on the additional work because they feel a sense of responsibility to their unit or institution or those who will benefit

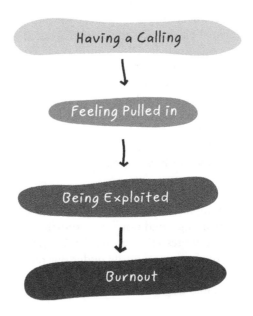

Figure 5.1 Path of calling to exploitation to burnout

from the work (like colleagues or students), even if they are already stretched thin with other tasks.

Helping others is another example of a value that can be exploited by higher education. For example, I know several amazing academic staff who are always willing to help others. Many of them have a vast internal library of institutional knowledge, much of which might not even be related to their specific role. However, because they are so willing to help others and are sought after for their expertise, they can spend much of their workweek supporting others at the expense of their assigned duties or feel guilty if they say no to requests for help. Arguably, when this happens, their value has been pulled to an extreme that might not be workable for them.

There are several mechanisms that Kim and colleagues (2019) describe that enable passion exploitation. One such mechanism is the popularization of the idea that passionate people find joy in their work and thus enjoy doing additional work or would have volunteered had they been asked. Second, given that passion for work is allegedly enjoyable, the additional work itself can be framed as a reward. We might assume that someone passionate about the work receives nontangible benefits (like joy) from doing additional work and thus does not need tangible benefits like extra pay or other forms of compensation.

Staying in the Realm of Workability

In the previous sections of this chapter, we've identified some places our values can take us (or ways others can use our values to exploit us) that are no longer workable for us. The core question from Acceptance and Commitment Therapy to identify workability is this: "Is what you're doing working to give you a rich, full, and meaningful life?" If you can answer yes to that question, you're still in what I like to call the "realm of workability" (recognizing that workability is a spectrum, not a binary). If the answer is no, then what you are doing is no longer workable. Figure 5.2 illustrates this balance.

Identifying workability can be easier said than done, however. For example, the core values that I have regarding mentoring and teaching others can make it very difficult for me to decline requests for help, even when my mental health is suffering. Saying yes is not workable in that context, but saying no is agonizing via the difficult emotions and thoughts that arise. Ironically, when we are in a place of wellness, it can be easier to protect our boundaries and, thus, that wellness. When we are overwhelmed or burnt out, it can be hard to set boundaries just when we need them the most.

Fortunately, you already know some strategies you could use to identify if something is workable for you. They are the same strategies we covered in Chapter 2 when we discussed identifying our values. Attention to our emotions, bodies, thoughts, and physiological reactions is a good way to notice workability. For example, helping someone else from a place of having enough capacity to do so often feels much more rewarding than when we push through the wall of burnout to do the same behavior. Carefully sitting down to ask

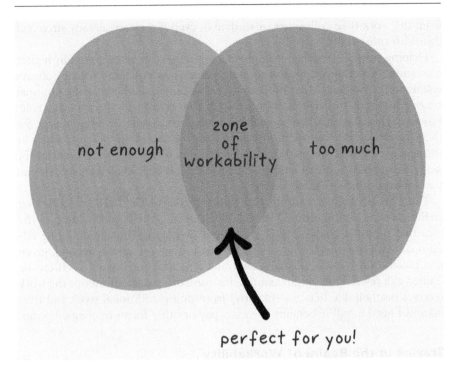

Figure 5.2 The realm of workability

ourselves the magic question, "Is what I'm doing working to give me a rich, full, and meaningful life?" and being compassionate but realistic in our answer is another great strategy. Last, surrounding ourselves with like-minded others is an excellent strategy for valued living in general. When evaluating workability, those around us who care about us and our self-care and well-being can be a great source of information. Asking someone else (like our N Committee) if a choice seems workable from their perspective is another excellent source of information.

Because we haven't mentioned the infamous "You're the boss, applesauce" in a little while, let me remind you that **workable is an entirely personal decision.** No one else can ultimately decide what is workable for you, and no one else needs to understand why something is workable for you. Remember as well, that your choices and behaviors are morally neutral.

Institutional Betrayal Trauma

When you identify your values and then derive your self-care and approach to work from them, you might discover that some of your core values do not match those expressed by higher education institutions. You might even find that your values conflict with those held by higher education. And whatever emotions that brings up for you – such as sadness, grief, or anger – are completely fine. I encourage you to make space for them. I also want to assure you that you are not alone.

There is a particular type of trauma that arises from being betrayed by those who are supposed to look after us (i.e., betrayal trauma; Birrell & Freyd, 2006). Institutional betrayal trauma can also happen in organizations and institutions (Smith & Freyd, 2014). If we expect our institutions to care for our well-being and they violate this expectation, we can feel betrayed, isolated, and alone. For many of us with specific values, not being seen as valuable to our employer can be painful. This can be particularly painful if our work involves being asked or required to do things that conflict with those values. At the extreme, this is referred to as a moral injury. Moral injuries are defined by psychiatrist Jonathan Shay, credited with defining the term, as "a betrayal of what's right, by someone who holds legitimate authority, in a high stakes situation" (2014, p. 183). It's being asked, pressured, or demanded to behave (by a person in authority over us) in a way that violates our morals.

As Laksmin describes, "When you live inside social structures that make your life harder and force you to make morally impossible decisions, it's not for lack of trying that you feel despair – it's that those systems have betrayed you. In other words, this isn't our fault" (2023, p. 43).

For many of us, institutional betrayal was part of our experience in our organizations (as well as broader societal systems) during the early years of the COVID-19 pandemic. These betrayals happened through actions and inactions (Adams-Clark & Freyd, 2021). In a large survey of 663 higher education staff working in the UK (Hanna, Erickson, & Walker, 2023), over half felt that they had acted in ways during the COVID-19 pandemic that put their health and well-being at risk (e.g., being required to return to the office). Almost 38% of respondents reported having acted in ways that compromised their moral judgment. However, those who compromised their moral judgment also believed that "senior management were the most responsible for them acting in such ways, followed by the UK government" (p. 991). For example, one participant described being sent back to the office by administrators who continued to work at home. Sixty-one percent felt betrayed by senior management, and 80% of participants described higher education as being betrayed by the UK government during the pandemic (Hanna et al., 2023). In her 2020 New York Times editorial, Lakshmin

hypothesized that what we all had been calling burnout was actually something different – it was societal betrayal at its most disturbing level. Over the course of the pandemic, the more I heard my patients use the term burnout, the more I felt it did not capture the depth of the crisis they were describing.

She describes: "These were women who faced impossible choices: Sending their child to school and risking viral exposure or not showing up to work". Such choices can be core to institutional betrayal trauma.

Institutional betrayal in higher education can happen in many actions and inactions – both small and large. For example, institutions expect us to ruthlessly prioritize research or industry dollars at the expense of caring about teaching, let alone having sufficient time to do it well. Higher education can betray us when it sends messages devaluing what we do – for example, by using metrics that only make sense in "hard sciences" and then portraying work done in the social sciences and humanities as less impactful because the metrics don't fit. It happens when institutional reward structures prioritize maximizing outputs like papers and grants and implicitly demand that we cut corners to achieve this (e.g., slicing our research into least publishable units, neglecting students in our courses, or driving our graduate students to overwork). Institutional betrayal trauma can happen to graduate students who are unsupported when they have relational difficulties with faculty or advisors, with sessional lecturers whose contracts aren't renewed after many years of service to their employer, and with staff who tirelessly do their jobs then receive little support when they are burnt out.

Do We Attempt to Change the Institution?

Noticing these feelings of betrayal (if you are someone who has them) can be part of our journey when we begin to do values work and prioritize self-care. Fundamentally, valuing self-care and your well-being conflicts with higher education as an institution because, as an agent of extractive capitalism who subscribes to neoliberal values, self-care is anathema to it. When we discussed, earlier in this book, all the anti-self-care messages that higher education sends us, this was evident.

Following this realization, many of us are led to a dilemma: Do we attempt to change the institution?

No one can answer that question for you. **Only you know the workable answer for your life**. In the next chapter, we will talk about your zone of influence and how to be a model for change if you choose to be.

I also want to assure you that if you decide it is not workable to try to change your institution to be more what you want it to be (often kinder, more human, more accessible, more diverse), that's completely okay. I say that despite the next chapter in this book being all about how to influence the organizational culture around self-care. **Choosing to try to change the system and choosing not to are equally valid choices**. I firmly believe that you should only engage in behaviors to influence change in higher education if those behaviors are workable for you. We should not undermine our wellness to influence others. Doing so (e.g., not putting on our air mask first, using the clichéd flying example) reduces our ability to help others in the long run.

Jobs Are For Money, Everything Else is a Bonus

As discussed earlier in this chapter, our values and the concept of "having a call-ing" or wrapping our identities up in our higher education work can leave us at risk of negative consequences. To summarize, seeing something as our calling might lead us to, for example, undervalue the worth of our expertise and labor. Our values, particularly if we hold those around helping and giving, might be exploited by institutions such that we work more than is manageable (i.e., work-able) for us. This can leave us at risk of burnout and all its adverse outcomes.

Said differently, when we expect our jobs to meet our values and their as-sociated needs, we might be setting ourselves up for disappointment (at best) or burnout and exploitation (at worst).

The reality is that a job has one single purpose: To pay you money. (Robin & Dominguez, 2008). (See Figure 5.3). (For those grad students reading, your graduate degree will lead you to a job with a single purpose: Earning money).

Being paid money is the only characteristic of a job that distinguishes it from an interest, hobby, volunteer opportunity, foray, eat-pray-love-style adventure or any other label we might think of for things we do that do not result in be-ing paid money. If we think of our job as the only way to be who we are (i.e., "having a calling") or the sole way of meeting our core values, we become more likely to give more than is workable for us, stay in a toxic situation, or not put ourselves first.

This doesn't mean it doesn't feel pretty fantastic when we can align (even some of) our work with our core values, which is what a great deal of this book has been about. But we shouldn't rely on work to be the sole means by which we meet those values. We can allow our jobs to be … just a job.

Something extraordinary about values is that there are many contexts in which we can live a values-consistent life. If that means that we meet some of our values at work, that's a great bonus to having a job. It also means that any value we might not have met at work can be met elsewhere. Unfortunately,

Figure 5.3 The purposes of having a job

higher education loves the narrative of "having a calling" or academia being our "passion". Admittedly, it can be a challenge sometimes to stop trying to use work to fulfill our values. But, valued-living is not called "value-jobbing" for a reason. There is a vast world in which we can live in values-consistent ways. I hope that is especially reassuring for any readers who don't find many of their values met by work.

For example, let's return to some of my core values I've shared in this book so far. I've added a new one: Richness of Life, which I define as creating a life that reflects who I am and what I want, including a balance of comfort and joy and adventure, spaciousness to explore who I am, and creating generational wealth in terms of money, emotional regulation skills, and secure family attachments. It has related values of contentment, energy, health, love, and longevity.

In Table 5.1, I share some ways I strive to meet my values at work (some of which you've seen before):

Table 5.1 Ways Jorden Meets Their Values at Work

Core Value	How I Meet This Value at Work
Creating Beauty	Focus on projects and roles that allow me to bring my inquisitive nature and love of learning to the table, to create beautiful outputs. Outputs include everything from syllabi to journal articles and beyond
Connection (Interspecies, Human, & Nature)	People are more important than projects. Connect with others and provide support without sacrificing my health. Be generous and ferocious in my protection and promotion of those I mentor
Richness of Life	Continue my journey of minimizing the role of work in my life while maximizing the idea that life is holistic. Give myself permission to create a career based on comfort, ease, enjoyment, and spaciousness (such as white space in my calendar and not overworking). Enjoy the process of work just as much as the outcomes

Here are some specific examples of how I've pursued these values at work over the last few years. For example, regarding Creating Beauty this past year, my lab received funding from the Saskatchewan Health Research Foundation to create a podcast showcasing the work of Saskatchewan-based scholars researching trauma, violence, and abuse. We got to learn how to do something new (record and promote a podcast) and create a beautiful (and permanent) output in the process.

With regards to Richness of Life, I have been working steadily over the past two years – along with my "self-care team" of close friends, therapist, and life coaches – to recalibrate what is a reasonable workload for me as well as engaging in projects that are fun to work on in addition to what they generate as an output. For example, I am involved in multiple research collaborations that use my skills as a qualitative researcher – but the primary reason I said yes to them was to work with the cool and fun people who invited me. This also moves me toward my value of Connection, as I am now focused more on who I collaborate with than what the project is. I'm also learning how to support the careers of others (related to core values around mentorship and lifting up others) without sacrificing myself along the way.

I am very fortunate to have the power and flexibility to pursue many of my values in my work in higher education. But because jobs are primarily for money, it's also important that I not put all of my values eggs in one values basket. First, doing so would encourage me to center my entire life around work – and this is not a workable situation for me. Second, as someone prone to workaholic tendencies, having a more holistic focus keeps me balanced. Last, goodness forbid I left or lost my job – not only would that cost me the financial security my personality craves…. I'd lose all the outlets to pursue the values that I had!

Instead, I can meet these values in other ways. Table 5.2 illustrates examples of how I meet the same values outside of work.

Table 5.2 Non-Work Ways I Meet My Values

Core Value	Non-Work Example(s) #1	Non-Work Example(s) #2
Creating Beauty	Continue to block off time to work on my hand-building skills using my pottery studio membership. Watch videos and try new projects	Foster a sense of playfulness and imagination in the everyday with my child. Slow down to be present and engage in creative play together (like drawing, storytelling, music, and building) weekly

(Continued)

Table 5.2 (Continued)

Core Value	Non-Work Example(s) #1	Non-Work Example(s) #2
Connection (Interspecies, Human, & Nature)	Engage in care activities with my cats on a regular basis. For example, ensure that we regularly groom them, play with them, and snuggle with them as much as possible. This includes my morning ritual of drinking tea while petting my cats and journalling	Teach generosity, reconciliation, peace, and sustainability practices to my child. Attend Indigenous and land-based learning opportunities as a family. Be present together in nature and share what we notice with one another
Richness of Life	Educate myself about ways to generate and share intergenerational wealth. Find ways to foster comfort at home. Manage my energy so that I have enough to give myself and my child, and make lifestyle decisions that are sustainable long-term	Create spaciousness for dream and thinking time daily by journalling, daydreaming, and reading about important topics and fiction that captivate me

"Diversifying" my valued-living portfolio not only focuses me on a holistic life that is workable, but it alleviates my previous stress about needing work to meet my values – and the disappointment, heartbreak, betrayal, and angst that resulted when it didn't. No value can only be met through a job. **Any value that you hold can be met in many ways beyond your career.** (And sometimes, the ways we pursue them *outside* of work or through our self-care practices are much more workable and create more joy than how we can get these needs met in our higher education careers).

Admittedly. I have had to work hard to accept that a job is just a way to be paid money. Ever since I was an undergraduate student, I bought heavily into the narrative that being a professor was a passion, a calling, and a way to serve some greater good in the world. By graduate school, I believed my skills and personality uniquely qualified me to be a professor. When I landed my tenure track job, it did not match all the values I brought with me (some of which I didn't even know yet). Because I believed in my "calling", the only assumption I could make when things didn't seem to be working out was that I was the problem. If my calling, passion, identity, and way to serve a greater good in the world was being a professor and I didn't like being a professor, I concluded that I was clearly a defective person. I thought I came off the professor assembly line with a defect, and I spent years trying to figure out what that defect might be – so that I could fix it, fit back in, and slog away for the remaining 35 years at my calling. After I began my obsession with "fixing" myself, my values of connection and integrity led me to overperform my work: Well past whatever was reasonable for any amount of money I have ever made.[1] Transitioning to accepting that work would not meet all of my values was an important step in ending this cycle of beating myself up and trying to "fix" myself by working too much (at the expense of my health and well-being).

Brainstorming other ways to pursue our values (including via our self-care) makes accepting that a job is just a job much, much easier. We can try to align our work with our values as much as possible, but we should also find other ways to live those values, especially those that might not be met by work at all.

A Note on Leaving Academia

Higher education is a challenging place to work. Remember that Tricia Hersey, the Nap Minister (2022), describes academia as the birthplace of grind culture. So many people leave academia that we even have a genre of writing about it: "quit lit". In a recent survey conducted at my institution, about 40% of faculty and 70% of lecturers reported that they have recently considered quitting their jobs!

You might be a higher education worker considering leaving academia, and that's okay. **There is no virtue to staying in higher education and no sin in leaving.** What matters is what is workable for you – to stay or to go is a morally neutral choice. Unfortunately, academia loves to send the message that those who leave are "weak", "not good enough", or "just couldn't cut it". This couldn't be further from the truth. If you're considering leaving, have left, or decide to leave, that's a perfectly workable decision.

Conclusion (TL;DR, But I Hope You Read)

This chapter focused on some dark sides of values, including taking our values to unhelpful (and unworkable) extremes, the possible dangers of pursing a

Figure 5.4 There are no choices in academia that are weak, only those that work or don't work for you

Photo by Arisa Chattasa, available on Unsplash at https://unsplash.com/photos/pair-of-pink-boxing-gloves-HZbqhd5aK3I

"calling" in our careers, and how this might leave us at risk of exploitation at work, and institutional betrayal trauma. We debated the pros and cons of working to change our institutions, and I noted that only you know if this is a workable choice for you – and that both choices are equally valid. I noted that jobs are ultimately for money and that we can pursue our values in many other aspects of our lives; we don't have to rely on our careers to meet our values. I shared some examples of how I meet my values outside of work. I concluded this chapter with a short note for anyone considering quitting higher education altogether.

Note

1 And if you're salaried, overworking brings you zero financial benefit if we adopt the "it's just a job" approach. Financially, there is no reason to work extra. That's probably the topic of another book.

References

Adams-Clark, A. A., & Freyd, J. J. (2021). COVID-19-related institutional betrayal trauma associated with trauma symptoms among undergraduate students. *PLoS ONE, 16*(1), e0258294. https://doi.org/10.1371/journal. pone.0258294

Bailey, C. (2016). *The productivity project*. Random House Canada.

Bailey, C. (2022). *How to calm your mind*. Random House Canada.

Birrell, P. J., & Freyd, J. J. (2006). Betrayal trauma: Relational models of harm and healing, *Journal of Trauma Practice, 5*, 49–63. https://doi.org/10.1300/J189v05n01_04

Cardador, M. T., & Caza, B. B. (2012). Relational and identity perspectives on healthy versus unhealthy pursuit of callings, *Journal of Career Assessment, 20*, 338–353. https://doi.org/10.1177/1069072711436162

Duffy, R. D., Allan, B. A., Autin, K. L., & Bott, E. M. (2013). Calling and life satisfaction: It's not about having it, it's about living it, *Journal of Counseling Psychology, 60*, 42–52. https://doi.org/10.1037/a0030635

Edwards, G. (March 26, 2013). 5 reasons to consider a career in higher ed. USA TODAY. Retrieved January 26, 2024, from https://www.usatoday.com/story/news/nation/2013/03/26/consider-a-career-in-higher-ed/2022195/

Gazica, M. W., & Spector, P. E. (2015). A comparison of individuals with unanswered callings to those with no calling at all, *Journal of Vocational Behavior, 91*, 1–10. https://doi.org/10.1016/j.jvb.2015.08.008

Hanna, P., Erickson, M., & Walker, C. (2023). UK higher education staff experiences of moral injury during the COVID-19 pandemic, *Higher Education, 86*, 985–1002. https://doi.org/10.1007/s10734-022-00956-z

Hartnett, S., & Kline, F. (2005). Preventing the fall from the 'call to teach': Rethinking vocation, *Journal of Education and Christian Belief, 9*, 9–20. https://doi.org/10.1177/205699710500900103

Hersey, T. (2022). *Rest is resistance: A manifesto*. Little Brown Spark.

Honor Society (April 19, 2023). Why working in higher education is a rewarding career choice. Retrieved January 26, 2024, from https://www.honorsociety.org/articles/why-working-higher-education-rewarding-career-choice

Kim, J. Y., Campbell, T. H., Shepherd, S., & Kay, A. C. (2019). Understanding contemporary forms of exploitation: Attributions of passion serve to legitimize the poor treatment of workers, *Journal of Personality and Social Psychology, 118*, 121–148. https://doi.org/10.1037/pspi0000190

Lakshmin, P. (2023). *Real self-care*. Penguin Random House.

Rawat, A., & Nadavulakere, S. (2015). Examining the outcomes of having a calling: Does context matter? *Journal of Business Psychology, 30*, 499–512. https://doi.org/10.1007/s10869-014-9378-1

Robin, V., & Dominguez, J. (2008). *Your money or your life*. Penguin.

Ruiz-Alfonso, Z., & Léon, J. (2016). The role of passion in education: A systematic review, *Educational Research Review, 19*, 173–188. https://doi.org/10.1016/j.edurev.2016.09.001

Shay, J. (2014). Moral injury, *Psychoanalytic Psychology, 31*, 182–191. https://doi.org/10.1037/a0036090

Smith, C. P., & Freyd, J. J. (2014). Institutional betrayal, *American Psychologist, 69*, 575–587. https://doi.org/10.1037/a0037564

Vallerand, R. J., Paquet, Y., Phillippe, F. L., & Charest, J. (2010). On the role of passion for work in burnout: A process model, *Journal of Personality, 78*, 289–312. https://doi.org/10.1111/j.1467-6494.2009.00616.x

Yukhymenko-Lescroart, M. A., & Sharma, G. (2019). The relationship between faculty members' passion for work and well-being. *Journal of Happiness Studies*, 20, 863–881. https://doi.org/10.1007/s10902-018-9977-z

Yukhymenko-Lescroart, M. A., & Sharma, G. (2020). Examining the factor structure of the revised sense of purpose scale (SOPS-2) with adults, *Applied Research Quality Life*, 15, 1203–1222. https://doi.org/10.1007/s11482-019-09729-w

Chapter 6

Changing Organizational Self-Care Culture

In the very first chapter of this book, I spoke about how the stress of working in higher education is a feature, not a bug. Higher education is part of extractive capitalism, a system that is a source of oppression for many of us who don't fit the mold of who academia was made for (white, rich, heterosexual, able-bodied men with stay-at-home wives or no family obligations). At the system and organizational levels, self-care is not valued (even though, ironically, it would likely make most of us more productive employees). Most institutions, and higher education as a whole, convey that your wellness is your problem. As Lakshmin notes, "Our culture has taken wellness and foisted it on the individual – where it can be bought, measured, and held up as personal success – instead of investing in making our social systems healthy" (2023, p. 5). This includes the culture of academia.

Thankfully, that's not good enough for many of us. We're not willing to be ground down into burnt-out husks of who we are for academia. Many people working in higher education are trying to change the system. After you build your self-care practices, I hope you will consider joining them and begin working to change higher education's attitude toward self-care.[1] After all, "a system changes only after a crucial mass of individual people show up differently" (Lakshmin, 2023, p. 203).

Self-Care as Labor Activism in Higher Education

It's probably no surprise at this point in the book for me to say that "self-care" is a term that gets a mixed reception within higher education. This is partly due to the commodification of self-care, which makes many of us feel understandably quite cynical about self-care advice. Commodified versions of self-care pushed on us by social media (a form of extractive capitalism) and completely disconnected from the real problems and stressors we experience in the workplace can make us feel cynical. Spending our money on face masks and remodeling our homes to match the latest trends does not address systematic inequities and ways that higher education mistreats us. We know the ways

DOI: 10.4324/9781003379805-7

we spend our salary mitigating the harms of work in higher education (e.g., for me, it's way more massages and physiotherapy than my benefits cover to deal with the chronic neck pain I've earned along with tenure and promotion) are unfair. But self-care is so much more than bubble baths and soothing. "Self-care" is a powerful label. Don't let capitalism remove the importance of self-care from our vocabulary. People often challenge me to use a different phrase, but these are the reasons I will be sticking with "self-care" for now: It's an act of reclaiming and resisting commodification.

Regarding oppressive and extractive systems and institutions, having a labor force that does not engage in self-care is in their best interests. Remember: The systematic problems with academia have been known for decades. They are a feature, not a bug. Overworked, exhausted, burnt out, and fried employees don't push back. They don't attend meetings unrelated to their direct tasks (like collegial governance), don't join their unions, don't have time to push back, and are too exhausted to organize. As Lakshmin eloquently describes,

> …yet the people at the bottom don't have time or mental energy to fight back or to change how they interact or question why things are done the way they are done. This is how oppressive systems work and the way they stay functioning.
>
> (2023, p. 54).

In this context, self-care becomes a powerful act of labor activism. First, just engaging in self-care and – even better, if you can – telling people about it challenges the dominant narrative in higher education that self-care is not something "dedicated" people engage in. The more we see people who engage in self-care, whose careers have not tumbled down around them in failure, the more we feel like maybe we can do self-care and have a career at the same time too. The more we see people who value their wellness, the more we think we can prioritize it too.

Engaging in self-care involves pushing back against the narrative that we must do nothing but work. It pushes back against the extractive capitalism of higher education – saying no, you will not get all the hours of my life. These are powerful acts of labor activism. "Learning to self-validate and overcome internalized stigmatization is extremely helpful in combating the damage of toxic messaging from the dominant culture" (Kinsey, 2022, p. 29). That is, engaging in self-care, as Audre Lorde said, is in and of itself an act of resistance.

Self-care can also create the physical and emotional space and energy for us to get involved in changing higher education. When we are well, we have the energy to listen to and support colleagues who need us. We have the extra time to join our union or organize. We have the rest and healthy stores of energy we need to speak up in a meeting and say, "This is an unreasonable workload" or "I am uncomfortable with this". Self-care enables acts of resistance by giving us the personal (and collective) resources we need to do it.

Self-care often creates pleasure, and "… pleasure evokes change – perhaps more than shame. More precisely, where shame makes us freeze and try to get really small and invisible, pleasure invites us to move, to open, to grow" (brown, 2017, p. 21). In *Emergent Strategy*, adrienne marie brown discusses how pleasure is demonized. This applies to higher education, where our worth is tied to what we produce rather than other metrics we might value, like how balanced we feel, our quality of life, or what pleasure we might take in our work. I encourage you to take a moment to imagine what your career might look like if your primary goal was to have fun rather than to fight against a scarcity of resources to produce more and more.

Top-Down (Institutional) vs. Bottom-Up (Grassroots) Change

One of the perks of being known in your circle of colleagues and friends as an anti-capitalist self-care researcher is the number of examples I get sent of tone-deaf institutions and employers "promoting self-care" for their employees. These include all of the memes about employers providing free pizza lunches for their staff, parody videos of people buying skin care products to ease the personal burden of working 16-hour days, bowls of rocks painted with encouraging messages for nurses (the message there being that the nurses rock) and – my favorite – a workplace that distributed (free) potatoes. The potatoes are so nonsensical that I can't remember why they were given out.

These remind me of one of my favorite pins on my backpack from the (unfortunately, now defunct) Little Science Co.: "Please don't empower me, just pay me".

Yes, #NotAllInstitutions are confusing (or confused?) when promoting employee self-care practices. An excellent example is Dan Price, CEO of Gravity Payments, who in 2015 raised the minimum salary for all employees at his company to $70,000/year. This was covered a fair bit in North American business news. As of the time I'm writing this book, Gravity Payments is still chugging along, and there are also many news stories of the benefits Dan Price's employees have reaped from their pay increase.

But of course, taking wellness practices for staff and faculty seriously is challenging when they come from higher education institutions we see as hypocritical. Those who don't hire enough administrative staff to support the work or rely primarily on precarious sessional teaching that doesn't require them to pay any benefits. We can't take seriously the anti-racism messaging of institutions where our colleagues are openly racist and sexist with no consequences, and we see minority colleagues leaving in droves. As the purpose of capitalism is to extract more and more labor (and profit) from us, of course, we are skeptical of institutional wellness plans. Often, any formal effort to boost our wellness seems meant to boost our productivity (and thus our organization's profits).

Do I hope there comes a day in higher education when we can receive our employers' wellness programming with nothing but feelings of sincerity? That would be fantastic. But I don't think that day is here yet.

In the meantime, we must rely upon bottom-up (grassroots) self-care movements in higher education. When we think grassroots, I love this definition from Wikipedia:

> use collective action from the local level to implement change at the local, regional, national, or international levels. Grassroots movements are associated with bottom-up, rather than top-down decision-making, and are sometimes considered more natural or spontaneous than more traditional power structures.
>
> (Grassroots, 2023).

Grassroots change is brought about by the people who need it, supporting other people in ways that match their actual needs (i.e., not their employers' needs). This is critical for making higher education a place where self-care is welcomed in the spaces and circles we need. Moreover, we all have a zone of influence where we can promote self-care for ourselves and others. Every single one of us can make a difference – and then, consistent with our labor activism/organization values, we can hopefully begin to influence our institutions more systematically. It takes a village to create a tipping point.

Where is Your Zone of (Self-Care) Influence?

Regardless of where we fall on the academic hierarchy (higher education loves its hierarchies!), we all have a zone of (self-care) influence. We all have people impacted by us – some known and some unknown.

To identify our zone of influence, we can ask ourselves: Who listens to me? (either because they choose to or because they have to). My students in my classes listen to me; it's part of them taking my classes. The students in my lab listen to me while completing their graduate degrees. My colleagues listen to me – some a fair bit and others only when it is my turn to speak in a meeting, and they are forced to. On social media, people who choose to follow me listen to me. My subscribers to the Rebel Scholar Dispatch on Substack listen to me. If you've made it this far in the book, you're listening to me, I hope.

Every one of us working in higher education has people who listen to us; those are the people we influence. Your zone of influence might be larger (say, if you're a University Provost) or smaller (say, if you're a graduate student TA), but it's there. Sometimes it's through what we say (and don't say), and sometimes it is through what we do (or don't). Sometimes we know we are influencing, and other times we aren't even aware. We influence those observing us, without our awareness, or through word of mouth about us.

Something promising for self-care progress in our zones of influence is that human behavior is contagious. There are decades of studies demonstrating how we influence one another. Examples of contagious human behavior include yawning (Franzen, Maden, & Winter, 2018), emotions (Herrando & Constantinides, 2021), exercise (Aral & Nicolaides, 2017), smoking, cooperation, and happiness (Christakis & Fowler, 2012), finance (Hirshleifer & Teoh, 2009), and public opinion (Krassa, 1988). This is such great news for self-care, as it's more evidence that demonstrates how impactful grassroots change (i.e., using our zone of influence) can be. Anecdotally, I can confirm that surrounding yourself with people who share your values (like wanting to engage in self-care) makes it much easier to engage in values-consistent behavior. The strength of our movement is "in the strength of our relationships" (brown, 2017, p. 10).

Figure 6.1 Surrounding yourself with people who share your values makes it easier to pursue those values

Photo by Tim Marshall, available on Unsplash at https://unsplash.com/photos/hands-formed-together-with-red-heart-paint-cAtzHUz7Z8g

Being A Self-Care Role Model

There are myriad ways that we can each be a self-care role model within our zone of influence.

Talk About Self-Care

Speaking truth to power is an impactful way to instigate change. One strategy available to many of us is simply to talk about self-care. Talk about the self-care we do, the self-care we wish we could do, the barriers to being able to do self-care, and how we can change things. Talk about our struggles and our successes. Hearing others speak about self-care tells us – even if we don't speak back – that considering our self-care is acceptable. Moreover, sometimes we learn strategies from others, including what to do and what *not* to do. Talking about something normalizes it.

If we don't hear anything being spoken around us about a challenge like self-care in higher education, this leads us to assume we're the problem. We can further internalize that we're the only one who struggles with self-care in higher education. That is, if the voices we hear never mention self-care, this reinforces the idea that *we* are the problem (when the problem is higher education).

Talking about self-care is an essential signal to others that self-care is important. It's like a specific bat signal[2] that tells the people around you that you're a safe space for self-care. By speaking about self-care, including your own experiences, you will continue to swim upstream in the face of academia's anti-self-care currents. Moreover, in my experience, you will draw others to you who also value self-care, which gives you a support network of like-minded people. It's like having a secret self-care handshake for those in the "self-care club". Except it's not secret because you're talking about it.

When I encourage people to talk about self-care, I often receive pushback from people who feel they don't have "enough" of a handle on their self-care to speak about it. My loving and supportive response to this is: That's wrong! To speak about it, you do not have to have your self-care perfectly figured out (spoiler alert: There is no such thing). Hearing about your challenges and your struggles might help someone else. If we all wait until we have perfect self-care to discuss self-care.... We will perpetuate the problem of no one ever hearing about self-care! I have been told more times than I can count that hearing about my struggles and journey with self-care has made someone else in higher education feel seen and not alone.

Talking about self-care includes asking questions and challenging assumptions influencing our struggles in higher education. In my opinion two statements alone are responsible for the bulk of dysfunctional tradition in higher education: "Because that's the way it's always been done" and "Because that's how we do it". (Note the lack of critical thinking in both statements.)

These assumptions interfere with our ability, and the abilities of others in higher education, to look after ourselves and experience wellness. Be the person who asks why. Why does this committee require evening or (goodness forbid) weekend meetings? Why does this service activity not have any credit attached to it? Why do we have meetings at the time my children need to be picked up from school? Why do we evaluate our students using this (stressful) method when we could use a much less stressful way? These are only some of the questions that come to mind.

Sometimes talking about self-care involves being willing to have hard conversations with no clear answers to our problems. There are legitimate barriers in higher education that interfere with our well-being (and the well-being of others). For example, in Canada, an important (and overdue) conversation occuring in academia is how we can decolonize our practices and work toward (re)conciliation with Indigenous Peoples. The education system in Canada has been more than oppressive for Indigenous Peoples; it has perpetrated cultural genocide (and outright genocide) through the residential school system and its support for other colonial practices. However, colonial violence is not a historical issue. It is a current issue as well. Our efforts to decolonize higher education should prioritize the voices of Indigenous Peoples themselves. And we must do this in a way that does not overburden Indigenous students, staff, and faculty, appropriate their knowledge, or interfere with their success. For example, Indigenous faculty are burdened with a much higher rate of service invitations than white faculty, which can interfere with their ability to be successful in tenure and promotion processes. How do we balance wanting to decolonize our institutions with not overburdening Indigenous faculty? I don't quite know – but that doesn't mean it isn't a critical conversation to have so that my Indigenous colleagues can be successful and not burnt out.

Adopt Creative Hopelessness

Having hard conversations is just the beginning of influencing self-care in our zones of influence and, ultimately, our organizations. At some point, we will likely feel compelled or be asked to solve self-care-related problems. Or, when we challenge those who use "Because this is the way we do it" or "It's always been done this way" they might (I hope) inevitably turn to us and say: "Okay, how do you think we should do it then?"

Creative hopelessness is a wonderful Acceptance & Commitment Therapy strategy that means acknowledging what we have tried has not worked even when we are unsure what to try next (Hayes, Strosahl, & Wilson, 2012). Adopting creative hopelessness means accepting that we might not know what to do in a particular situation but that we know what we've been trying hasn't worked. When we give up on what hasn't worked, we create space for new strategies to emerge. Admittedly, the use of "hopeless" here can be misinterpreted as something negative. As Hayes and colleagues note, "The goal is not to elicit a *feeling* of hopelessness or a *belief* in hopelessness; instead, the objective is to give up strategies when [our experience] *says they do not work*, even if what comes next is not yet known" (Hayes et al., 2012, p. 190). "It is a generative, self-affirming act, and the feeling state that comes along with it is often a kind of ironic hopefulness or an anticipation of new possibilities" (p. 190).

Asking ourselves, "How can this be done?" (which has a multitude of answers and lends itself to brainstorming solutions) instead of "Can this be done?" (which only has two answers: Yes and no) is a great way to begin using creative hopelessness to our advantage.

Instead of asking ourselves and others, "Can we do this in a way that promotes self-care?" which implies that we might not be able to, and maybe self-care isn't even that important anyway, asking, "How can we do this in a way that promotes self-care?" is a much more flexible way to approach issues of balance and wellness. This question intrinsically values self-care – it is not debating whether self-care should be promoted but asks how we will do it. How can we teach our classes in a way that promotes self-care? How can we run our departments and collegial processes, hire and support junior colleagues, lobby against tenuous employment, not overburden staff, and conduct our scholarship in ways that promote self-care? We don't have to know the answers yet, but asking ourselves questions phrased to engage our problem-solving skills is a great way to begin working toward them. And we don't have to have "right" answers, just workable ones.

Be a Self-Care "People Leader"[3] by Walking the Walk (Change What You Can)

If we truly value self-care and want to create space for change in higher education, we need to be a People Leader[3] who actively promotes the self-care of those we oversee, manage, lead, teach, and mentor. **We cannot think self-care is great for us but not for the people we work with**. We need to be a rising (self-care) tide that lifts all (self-care) boats. We need to walk the walk of valuing self-care within our organizations, not just talk the talk.

This means ensuring that the people we directly influence (i.e., those whose work we are responsible for, like our students) feel supported in their self-care. I guarantee you that the odds are likely you will be the only person doing so, and they really, really need you.

We cannot claim to value self-care and then assign students in our class more readings and assignments than they can complete in one week. We cannot claim that we want higher education to have space for balance if we expect our research assistants to work every evening and weekend and respond to our emails within 15 minutes, no matter when we send them. Or think that it's great for us to have hobbies and interests but that the graduate students in our programs must sacrifice all their lives if they are "serious about their training". Or that it's okay for us to have reasonable teaching schedules while at the same time precariously employed sessional lecturers in our department (Do you know who your sessional lecturers are?) receive no compensation for their prep time, no office, and no benefits.

(Are you feeling uncomfortable? If you're having a "but this is how it's always been done" moment, great job noticing that discomfort. I encourage you to pause and reflect on that. No judgment – this thinking in higher education is a feature, not a flaw, and it's hard to de-program ourselves from how we were socialized. We can only de-program if we notice and challenge the reactions that arise for us. So really, great noticing).

Walking the walk as a People Leader who values self-care means facilitating wellness for those we manage. It means confirming that they aren't working 24/7, making sure they get to take a vacation, and that they stay home when they are sick (among many other things). It means checking in on how they are doing.

The people that I most directly People-Lead are the graduate students and research assistants who work under my supervision, and students in classes I teach. Here are some examples of how I and others I know in similar roles have shown up for their students and other trainees/staff in ways to promote self-care:

- Structuring training opportunities so time off is built in.
- Having a lab policy of when students are expected to be on email (For example, in my lab no one is expected to reply to an email in the evening or on weekends except for in very rare circumstances and with warning. This *might* happen once a year at most).
- Creating thesis and dissertation projects that are manageable in scope but still rigorous enough to succeed.
- Checking in with everyone's well-being at the start of meetings. Having meeting ice breakers that center self-care ("What's one thing you're going to do this week for self-care?").
- Creating lab values and lab policies related to respectful and kind interactions with one another.
- Having ceremonies and traditions to celebrate student accomplishments.
- Halving the number of readings in my syllabus.
- Providing students with time in class for assignment work.
- Always saying yes (within reason and my limits) to requests for extensions on course assignments or building in flexible deadlines.

These are only some ways you might facilitate the self-care of others you oversee. Remember, a key question is, "How can this be done (in a way that promotes self-care)?"

Don't forget those nurses and their basket of rocks or the potatoes handed out for reasons I can't remember.[4] The take-home message being: If you talk the talk but don't follow through in your behavior (or give your trainees rocks), everyone will quickly know you don't *really* care about their self-care. After that, no one will listen to you (nor should they, frankly).

Respect Diversity in Self-Care Choices

As I've said a lot during this book, just like people are different and have different values, there is infinite variety in what self-care works for different people. If we want to be a good self-care role model, we must accept this diversity. Said differently, people might benefit greatly from self-care practices we don't necessarily understand. Being a good self-care role model means accepting that.

For example, one surefire way to stir up people in higher education regarding self-care is to discuss whether we should send emails outside of business hours. Many people believe we should only send emails during business hours, which is the best way to promote self-care around email. These people also argue that even if we explicitly tell others that receiving an email from us outside of regular business hours doesn't mean we expect a reply outside those hours, we are still pressuring them to reply. Other people say that responding to their emails on their schedule is their self-care and that if someone takes the time to tell us when they expect a reply or don't, we need to believe them. This is yet another example of how we cannot prescribe particular behaviors as self-care, how we must consider the function of a behavior and if it replenishes the person choosing to do it, and how self-care choices are idiosyncratic.

Conclusion (TL;DR, But I Hope You Read)

In this chapter, we discussed how self-care is a vital form of labor activism in self-care. Moreover, being well places us in a better position to be involved in changing our systems and institutions, should we choose to do so. Self-care is a critical form of pleasure activism. I reviewed top-down (institutional) versus bottom-up (grassroots) change. We considered what your zone of self-care influence might be and reviewed strategies for being a self-care role model for those in that zone of influence.

Notes

1 But, as mentioned in the previous chapter, if you choose not to try to change academia that's a completely acceptable choice too!
2 Used to summon Batman, for those of you who might not be familiar with the term "bat signal".
3 "People Leader" is my institution's label of choice for person who oversees others aka manager. Here I use the term to refer to both those we formally manage and those we might informally influence.
4 Yes, I tried to google this but nothing useful came up except a few delicious potato recipes.

References

Aral, S., & Nicolaides, C. (2017). Exercise contagion in a global social network, *Nature Communications, 8*, 14753. https://doi.org/10.1038/ncomms14753

brown, am (2017). *Emergent strategy*. AK Press.

Christakis, N. A., & Fowler, J. H. (2012). Social contagion theory: Examining dynamic social networks and human behavior, *Statistics in Medicine, 32*, 556–577. https://doi.org/10.1002/sim.5408

Franzen, A., Mader, S., & Winter, F. (2018). Contagious yawning, empathy, and their relation to prosocial behavior, *Journal of Experimental Psychology: General, 147*, 1950–1958. https://doi.org/10.1037/xge0000422

Grassroots. (2023, December 20). In *Wikipedia*. https://en.wikipedia.org/wiki/Grassroots

Hayes, S. C., Strosahl, K. D., & Wilson, K. G. (2012). *Acceptance and commitment therapy* (2nd ed.). Guilford.

Herrando, C., & Constantinides, E. (2021). Emotional contagion: A brief overview and future directions. *Frontiers in Psychology, 12*, 712606. https://doi.org/10.3389/fpsyg.2021.712606

Hirshleifer, D., & Teoh, S. H. (2009). Thought and behavior contagion in capital markets. In T. Hens, & K. R. Schenk-Hoppé (Eds.), *Handbook of financial markets: Dynamics and evolution* (pp. 1–56). Elselvier.

Kinsey, D. K. (2022). *Decolonizing wellness*. BenBella Books, Inc.

Krassa, M. A. (1988). Social groups, selective perception, and behavioral contagion in public opinion, *Social Networks, 10*(2), 109–136. https://doi.org/10.1016/0378-8733(88)90018-4

Lakshmin P. (2023). *Real self-care*. Penguin Random House.

Conclusion

I'm ending the first draft of this book on an unseasonably warm Winter day. After two weeks of deep freeze, the sudden warmth triggered a fog that lasted well into the afternoon and a beautiful hoarfrost. Having come out to Wanuskewin Heritage Park for a meeting today, I decided to stay and write in the restaurant for the afternoon. In a few hours, I will return to the city to pick up my child from school and resume being "Mommy" instead of "Professor". Driving into the park, the buffalo herd was right along the road – I've never seen them up close despite having been here many times. I considered this an auspicious start to the day.

I hope we are reaching a tipping point in higher education where enough people value wellness, balance, and living a holistic life that we will see a more vocal and obvious shift toward valuing (loudly!) self-care. Every one of us deserves well-being and a life worth living simply by being alive. None of us must earn this.

In this book, I introduced you to the ideas around self-care in higher education that I have been developing and researching for over a decade. I shared with you an anti-capitalist, self-care-as-activism approach that encourages you to take charge of your self-care AND your career for the sake of your health. I am confident, based on the feedback I've received from so many others during this journey, that I am "on to something". Likewise, I know my thinking will continue to develop and be refined. I hope you have found the strategies in this book helpful, but more importantly, I hope you take away any permission you might need to build your life and career the way you want to. Remember: You're the boss, applesauce! There are no right or wrong choices, only those that are workable and those that are not.

Over the time I've spent writing this book, I've been introduced to the work of Shirley Turcotte and concepts of Indigenous Focusing-Oriented Therapy. I have been inspired by many reflections (too many for one conclusion). The one that stands out to me the most lately is the importance of love. The correlation between love and wellness, the role of love and its absence in higher education, and the power of love to make us feel validated and supported. So, I will conclude with love: I love you all! Good luck out there ☺

DOI: 10.4324/9781003379805-8

Wellbeing and Self-care in Higher Education
Editor: Narelle Lemon

Healthy Relationships in Higher Education
Promoting Wellbeing Across Academia
Edited by Narelle Lemon

In this edited collection, authors navigate how they view relationships as a crucial part of their wellbeing and acts of self-care, exploring the "I", "We", and "Us" at the centre of self-care and wellbeing embodiment.

Creating a Place for Self-care and Wellbeing in Higher Education
Finding Meaning Across Academia
Edited by Narelle Lemon

In this edited collection, the authors navigate how they find meaning in their work in academia by sharing their own approaches to self-care and wellbeing.

Creative Expression and Wellbeing in Higher Education
Making and Movement as Mindful Moments of Self-care
Edited by Narelle Lemon

This book focuses on the lived experiences of higher education professionals working in the face of stress, pressure and the threat of burnout and how acts of self-care and wellbeing can support, develop and maintain a sense of self.

Reflections on Valuing Wellbeing in Higher Education
Reforming our Acts of Self-care
Edited by Narelle Lemon

Designed to support readers working in higher education, this volume focuses on individual and collective practices of creativity, embodiment and movement as acts of self-care and wellbeing highlighting how connection to hand, body, voice and mind can be essential to this process.

Practising Compassion in Higher Education
Caring for Self and Others Through Challenging Times
Edited by Narelle Lemon, Heidi Harju-Luukkainen and Susanne Garvis

Presenting a collective international story, this book demonstrates the importance of compassion as an act of self-care in the face of change and disruption, providing guidance on how to cope under trying conditions in higher education settings.

Women Practicing Resilience, Self-care and Wellbeing in Academia
International Stories from Lived Experience
Edited by Ida Fatimawati Adi Badiozaman, Voon Mung Ling and Kiran Sandhu

Through a lens of self-care and wellbeing, this book shares stories of struggle and success from a diverse range of women in academia, illustrating the ways that higher education institutions can be more accommodating of the needs of women.

Writing Well and Being Well for Your PhD and Beyond
How to Cultivate a Strong and Sustainable Writing Practice for Life
Katherine Firth

Prioritizing wellbeing alongside academic development, this book provides practical advice to help students write well, and be well, during their PhD and throughout their career. Relevant at any stage of the writing process, this book will help doctoral students and early career researchers to produce great words that people want to read, examiners want to pass and editors want to publish.

Prioritising Wellbeing and Self-Care in Higher Education
How We Can Do Things Differently to Disrupt Silence
Edited by Narelle Lemon

This book illuminates international voices of those who feel empowered to do things differently in higher education, providing inspiration to those who are seeking guidance, reassurance, or a beacon of hope.

Navigating Tensions and Transitions in Higher Education
Effective Skills for Maintaining Wellbeing and Self-care
Edited by Kay Hammond and Narelle Lemon

With a focus on skills development, this book provides guidance on how to navigate transitions between career stages in higher education and how to maintain wellbeing in the process. Written with all career stages in mind, this book will be an essential resource for new and experienced researchers alike.

Sustaining Your Well-Being in Higher Education
Values-based Self-Care for Work and Life
Jorden Cummings

This book provides an evidence-based approach to sustainable self-care, anchoring these strategies in individual academics' core personal values. It teaches readers how to use their values to leverage self-care strategies into a workable, individualised, and effective map to wellness.

Passion and Purpose in the Humanities
Exploring the Worlds of Early Career Researchers
Edited by Marcus Bussey, Camila Mozzini-Alister, Bingxin Wang and Samantha Willcocks

In the spirit of guiding emerging researchers in higher education, this book features twenty unique essays by emergent scholars who weave their personal lives into their research passions, offering a window into the experience of researchers in both professional and personal developments.

Exploring Time as a Resource for Wellness in Higher Education
Identity, Self-care and Wellbeing at Work
Edited by Sharon McDonough and Narelle Lemon

Bringing together international perspectives, this book demonstrates the importance of reframing time in higher education and how we can view it as a resource to support wellbeing and self-care. Whether it's making time, having time, or investing in time, this book explores strategies and reflections necessary to grow, maintain, and protect wellbeing.

Innovative Practices for Supporting and Promoting Wellbeing in the Higher Education Sector
Institutional and Individual Perspectives of Wellbeing Initiatives and Innovations in Action
Edited by Angela R. Dobele and Lisa Farrell

This book examines academic wellbeing from both institutional and individual perspectives, highlighting innovative approaches to support and promote the psychological health of faculty in an increasingly volatile higher education landscape. Featuring evidence-based practices and firsthand accounts, the book equips readers with practical ideas and strategies they can implement to become wellbeing champions within their own workplaces.

Understanding Wellbeing in Higher Education of the Global South
Contextually Sensitive and Culturally Responsive Perspectives
Edited by Youmen Chaaban, Abdellatif Sellami and Igor Jacky Dimitri Michaleczek

This volume presents an alternative conceptualization of wellbeing in higher education, grounded in the socio-cultural context of the Global South. By delineating a contextually-sensitive and culturally-responsive perspective, the edited book challenges dominant Western notions of wellbeing and invites readers to explore the complexity and multi-dimensionality of this construct across diverse educational settings.

For more information about this series, please visit www.routledge.com/ Wellbeing-and-Self-care-in-Higher-Education/book-series/WSCHE

Index

For Product Safety Concerns and Information please contact our EU
representative GPSR@taylorandfrancis.com Taylor & Francis Verlag GmbH,
Kaufingerstraße 24, 80331 München, Germany

Printed and bound by CPI Group (UK) Ltd, Croydon, CR0 4YY

08/06/2025

01897006-0014